Praise for *After Sh*

"Kent Annan walks his readers through the rubble of the earthquake that hit Haiti unforgettably. I have known Kent for eight years since he and his wife first moved here to Haiti and lived with a family in the countryside to learn and experience Haitian life. *After Shock* tells the story of all of us who have lived through this terrible event."
Jean Claude Cerin, Tearfund Haiti

"Kent Annan struggles with his faith existentially. This is no simple attempt to excuse God for non-interference in the suffering that pervades Port-au-Prince following a devastating earthquake. Instead, it is the poetic confession of a Christian who faces his doubts and questions about God, and yet goes beyond them to find a newer, stronger faith."
Tony Campolo, Professor Emeritus, Eastern University

"Annan has put into words the questions many of us wrestle with in silence, and done so with such humanity and humility, it's impossible to walk away unchanged. This is a raw, beautiful and courageous book, brimming with truth on every page."
Rachel Held Evans, author of *Evolving in Monkey Town*

"Like Kent Annan, I've walked through the devastation of Port-au-Prince and its surrounding mountains in the wake of the January 2010 earthquake. Like Kent I've seen and smelled the tragedy, and shaking questions have met my soul. In *After Shock* he describes palpably how Christ's broken, resurrected body meets our brokenness in a tangible, fragile, personal way—a way so essential to a lasting faith. *After Shock* will summon you to a journey of real, vibrant, honest faith in the holy God who promises to be with us always, even in the bruised and broken circumstances of life."
Benjamin Homan, president of John Stott Ministries and former president of Food for the Hungry

"Page after page in *After Shock,* I've been blown away by Kent Annan's raw honesty, risky vulnerability and human sensitivity. On top of that there's his robust and clear writing style. And there's the simple fact of where he's been, what he's seen and felt, what he's asked and refused to accept, and how he's struggled to make sense of it all. It yields a rich book that has the chance, with your cooperation, to make you a better Christian, a better human being."

Brian McLaren, author/activist

"This is no ivory-tower exploration of faith and doubt. In *After Shock,* Kent Annan offers a muscular, gritty and devastatingly hopeful model of a faith lived between the questions. Like Haiti after the earthquake, it recoils from quick-fix inspiration or a sappy resolution. Instead it offers something much more powerful: truth."

Jason Boyett, author of *O Me of Little Faith* and *Pocket Guide to the Afterlife*

KENT ANNAN

AFTER SHOCK

SEARCHING FOR HONEST FAITH

WHEN YOUR WORLD IS SHAKEN

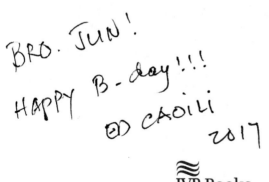

BRO. JUN!
HAPPY B-day!!!
⊕D CAOILI
2017

IVP Books

An imprint of InterVarsity Press
Downers Grove, Illinois

With gratitude to: Enel, Edvard, the Cadet and Auguste families, and many friends in Haiti. All who helped Mike and the Cadet family. The board, staff and supporters of Haiti Partners. All at InterVarsity Press. Dave Zimmerman, Kathy Helmers, Lisa, Tabitha, Doug, Adam and Owen, for improving this book. Shelly, my beautiful, patient, insightful partner in it all. Our beloved children, Simone and Cormac.

InterVarsity Press
P.O. Box 1400, Downers Grove, IL 60515-1426
World Wide Web: www.ivpress.com
Email: email@ivpress.com

InterVarsity Press® is the book-publishing division of InterVarsity Christian Fellowship/USA®, a movement of students and faculty active on campus at hundreds of universities, colleges and schools of nursing in the United States of America, and a member movement of the International Fellowship of Evangelical Students. For information about local and regional activities, write Public Relations Dept., InterVarsity Christian Fellowship/USA, 6400 Schroeder Rd., P.O. Box 7895, Madison, WI 53707-7895, or visit the IVCF website at <www.intervarsity.org>.

Scripture quotations, unless otherwise noted, are from the New Revised Standard Version of the Bible, copyright 1989 by the Division of Christian Education of the National Council of the Churches of Christ in the USA. Used by permission. All rights reserved.

While the stories in this book are about real events and people, some names and identifying details have been altered to protect their privacy.

Permission for previously published material has been requested.

Design: Cindy Kiple
Images: Devastated church, Darbonne, Haiti/David A. Zimmerman

ISBN 978-0-8308-3617-8

Printed in the United States of America ∞

Library of Congress Cataloging-in-Publication Data

Annan, Kent, 1973-
 After shock: searching for honest faith when your world is shaken /
by Kent Annan.
  p. cm.
Includes bibliographical references.
ISBN 978-0-8308-3617-8 (pbk.: alk. paper)
 1. Suffering—Religious aspects—Christianity. 2. Faith. I. Title.
BV4905.3.A55 2011
 231'.8—dc22

                                                                        2010033184

| **P** | 21 | 20 | 19 | 18 | 17 | 16 | 15 | 14 | 13 | 12 | 11 | 10 | 9 | 8 | 7 | 6 | 5 | 4 | 3 | 2 | 1 |
| **Y** | 29 | 28 | 27 | 26 | 25 | 24 | 23 | 22 | 21 | 20 | 19 | 18 | 17 | 16 | 15 | 14 | 13 | 12 | 11 |

CONTENTS

Tectonic Plates

Tectonic plates are the large, thin, rigid plates that move relative to one another near the outer surface of the earth. They usually move a few inches a year, about the rate hair grows.

But sometimes they get stuck. The stress builds until it releases, sending energy up through the earth's crust and shaking the surface. An earthquake.

Aftershocks are the smaller, follow-up jolts that occur as the tectonic plates get back in motion. They can occur for months or years after the main shock.

An average of 1 eight-plus-magnitude earthquake, 18 seven-plus earthquakes and 134 six-plus earthquakes happen each year. Several million occur annually, most of them small. Earthquake activity has remained steady for as long as it has been measured, though the increasing population means the shifting plates can result in more human casualties.

Our lives take place on an unstable planet.

◆　◆　◆

"Where were you?" I ask the Haitian teacher I've known for years. We're standing in the countryside near the epicenter of the 7.0 earthquake that devastated the country.

"I had just said goodbye to the children in my classroom and left school," she says. "I was walking through the field on my way home. I fell down. So did my friends. We were shocked but also laughed. Then I ran home. It collapsed but everyone was okay. But my aunt and two cousins were in the city. They were inside. They died."

"I'm so sorry."

"What about you, where were you?" she asks me.

"I was at home in Florida when it happened."

"I know. And what happened to your house there? Did it fall or is it okay?"

It takes me a second to realize that, yes, of course, to her in that moment it's like the *whole world* shook.

LIFE GETS SHAKEN

FOUR YEARS AGO, I walked to our car with six pounds, eight ounces pressed to my chest. A knit pink cap cradled Simone's downy head. It was September in North Dakota, where we'd been staying with my wife's family after pregnancy complications in Haiti. I floated on pride in my wife and new daughter, who made her first venture from the hospital into the world tucked inside my jacket so she wouldn't be touched by even a stiff wind.

(The contrasting memory comes to mind as I walk through a town outside Port-au-Prince and near the epicenter. Three friends told me during the day that they had lost children in or soon after the earthquake. One conversation beside a crumpled church, another in a dusty street, another next to three collapsed homes. Meanwhile little Mike was rescued and keeps holding on . . .)

With Simone snug in her car seat, I checked each way seven or eight times before pulling slowly onto the wide, quiet street. No head of state or loaded Briggs truck has been chauffeured with more care. My eyes scanned the road for broken glass, deer, shredded tire, buffalo.

Fifty yards ahead a car changed lanes without a blinker. I wanted to chase it down, throw the driver on the hood and scream: "You reckless psychopath! Don't you know how precious LIFE IS?" Then, after throwing his keys into the ditch, I'd walk him to our car, "Oh, do you see my new daughter? Can you believe that little nose, those long, thin fingers?"

Eyes, nose, ears, fingers, eyelashes, toes. This world is not fit for such perfection. In those first days of my daughter's life, everything felt more serious and meaningful. I'd never felt happier. I'd never felt such fear. My black and white turned to vivid color. Pixel density intensified exponentially. All the angles were sharper. The edge of a door could have cut a steak. The joy and fear danced together like faith and doubt.

If I'd been born in a different time or place, I could have done crazy things to appease whatever needed appeasing to ensure Simone's safety. Cut the throats of goats and bathe us in their blood. Repeat chants by ancient, drunken priests. Dance, strip, sacrifice, bleed, immerse, pilgrimage, drink, abstain.

Each time I rolled over in those first nights after she was born, both anxiety and my can't-stop-staring-at-her awe overcame exhaustion. I couldn't sleep again till I shuffled around the bed to put my hand on her chest. Up and down. So I could breathe again too. Her ribs curved like delicate twigs. Rest my hand there. I kept doing this ten times a night for weeks. Still breathing. I was grateful to the God whom I struggle to trust, knowing her breath could stop, knowing I couldn't trust the world into which she was born. For the first year I continued this several times each night—put my hand on her as a silent prayer, as an expression of doubt and gratitude for each breath moving in and out.

◆ ◆ ◆

My daughter Simone is four now, just a few months older than Gustave's son, Mike. Gustave has been watching carefully over each of Mike's breaths; it is a wonder he's still breathing at all.

Gustave has been a friend for eight years now, since my wife, Shelly, and I first moved to Haiti. We worked with Gustave in the same office, and he drove a taxi on the side. We also shared some adventures—like the time Shelly and I hired him to provide transportation for a group of visitors we were hosting, about a year after we arrived in Haiti. He drove us to the countryside in his pickup truck. On the way back, we had seven or eight flat tires. The last one happened in Port-au-Prince as the sun was setting.

Still relatively new in the city, we sat exposed in the back of Gustave's truck while he went in search of a new tire. Soon gunshots started popping nearby. Shelly and I were nervous—okay, verging on scared—but trying to act composed for the sake of our American guests. Gunshots echoed around us again. Then we noticed a TV flickering with a soccer match. The shots were goal celebrations (which was slightly comforting). After an hour Gustave returned and finally fixed the tire. As we approached home and normal breathing resumed, we were able to laugh about it together.

Gustave also helped us during volatile political times in Port-au-Prince. Sometimes he would volunteer to walk with us through the streets as informal security, or I would ask him to accompany Shelly to a meeting if I had to be elsewhere. We trusted him, even if we had significantly less confidence in his vehicle.

When the earthquake struck, Gustave was at home with Mike, his wife and one of his two daughters. They quickly ran out of their small concrete block home as it shook violently, managing to escape just before one of the walls collapsed.

After ensuring everyone was okay, Gustave tried to call the school where his eleven-year-old daughter, Carla, was. Impossible to get through, so he started running down one of the city's main streets toward where she was a couple of miles away.

He ran past the Caribbean Market, probably the best and largest grocery store in the country, seeing that it too had collapsed. Dozens of bodies were already lining the street. Sure that Carla must be dead downtown, he kept running. Running through waves of people covered in dust who were walking up the street in shock. Scanning for her white-and-green-striped uniform in the crowd. Losing hope along the way. Until finally he saw white and green. Yes, yes, it's her. He fell to his knees in the middle of the street, raised his hands and started to thank God with tears streaming down his cheeks.

Carla ran up and hugged him. "You don't have to cry, Dad. I'm okay, I'm okay."

Six days after the earthquake, Gustave was telling this to me and my friend and colleague John as we stood on a corner in Port-au-Prince. We talked about the mutual friends we'd heard from; we waited for news telling us whether others were alive. At the end of the conversation, Gustave said his son, Mike, was pretty sick. It had started before the earthquake but had gotten worse in the past few days. Any way we could help?

A few days later John arranged for Mike and Gustave to see a doctor. Gustave thought he was just taking Mike for quick care at one of the emergency tent hospitals. After a brief look at Mike, however, the doctors told Gustave he had to be taken with Mike to the airport immediately and get on a plane for medical evacuation to Miami. There was no time to go home to pack or say goodbye to his wife and two daughters. Now.

If they hadn't gotten on a plane then, if the doctors hadn't been there and the window for medical evacuations hadn't briefly opened because of the disaster, if treatment in the United States hadn't started immediately, Mike would have likely died "within a few days or a few weeks," his oncologist later told me. Mike had leukemia. The earthquake that had just killed about 230,001 saved his life.*

◆ ◆ ◆

The earthquake wiped out the equivalent of the population of Corpus Christi, Texas, in an instant. That's almost 100 times more deaths

---

*The number of people who died can only be estimated and so rounded off, but adding the one seems like a way to try to hold onto the personal scale of loss.

than 9/11 in a country that is only about 3 percent the population of the United States.

Elie Wiesel, who lived through the Holocaust and has written profoundly about it, says you must never compare tragedies. You don't say Stalin's massacre of four to ten million Russians was even worse than Hitler's massacre of six million Jews, or vice versa. You don't say that the genocide of x number of people wasn't as bad. Any statement that contains "logic" like this—only hundreds of thousands killed, not millions!—is absurd and dehumanizing. Such comparisons diminish those who faced the horrors. People deserve to be respected and remembered in the singularity of what they faced.

Wiesel is right, of course, and it's also true that some people's suffering is much more severe than others'. Haiti's really is incomparable. But in our own ways we each can face devastation and disappointment. Within the awful individuality of each instance of suffering, whether physical or existential or another kind, is something universally human. Life can crash quickly or slowly, visibly or invisibly: tsunamis and hurricanes and financial collapses, a doctor delivering a cancer diagnosis to a loved one, being laid off from a job, the betrayal of a spouse or girl- or boyfriend, an assault, a son in a fatal car accident.

God's children get crushed under the rubble—sometimes literally, sometimes figuratively—all the time.

I've worked with a nonprofit focused on education in Haiti for eight years, living there for two-and-a-half of them. While I wasn't in Port-au-Prince when the earthquake happened, I'd been there a few weeks before and flew down six days after. Following the earthquake, I'm shaken. I'm searching. People who claim definitive answers on faith, doubt and suffering can't be trusted. I'm not trying to convert you to faith or to some perspective. Not trying to be careful or right. Not proposing a new theodicy. I am trying to search honestly.

After 230,001 in a country I care deeply about were crushed, I'm not in the mood to praise God and barely in the mood to believe. But I'm not yet serving my divorce papers; my life feels so wrapped up in the meaning of Jesus Christ that I don't know that I could escape if I wanted to. "If I make my bed in Sheol, you are there," says the writer of Psalm 139.

If this book is written in a literary tradition, it's a psalm of lament that starts with pain and absence and tries to claw its way by the end to gratitude and faith.

In the weeks after the earthquake, it wasn't possible to slow down enough to ask the big questions. And I didn't want to. The *why* questions rightly got pushed aside by the *how* of helping. There were short prayers along the way. Most often for me it was the refrain in many psalms, "How long, O LORD? How long?" I'm still searching this question now. And it's not just about Haiti. It's about living in this world.

This book isn't a revelation brought down from a Himalayan mountaintop or a silent monastery retreat. I'm in the middle of a lot of work and little sleep. I'm bothered by difficult hiring decisions and budgeting issues as we try, in our small way, to respond to overwhelming needs in Haiti. I'm writing about faith but missed church on Sunday because our son had a fever. I had crazy heart palpitations (or something like that) and a sensation of being shaken as I tried to fall asleep, so I just got a prescription for Ambien to sleep better. I'm disappointing too many people. There are too many unanswered emails. There is so much more I could do to help.

My parents want me to call more often so they can talk with me—and, more importantly, with their grandchildren. The car engine light has been on for three weeks. The oil was due to be changed 1,462 miles ago. We have two kids and don't have a will (my mom is appalled in her gentle way). I could be a better husband and father;

my wife and children deserve that. I have so much to be grateful for but don't know that I manage it all well. To the prophet Elijah, God appeared as a gentle whisper. That's great, but I'm also counting on appearances coming in the cacophony of life.

The search for faith is mysterious but also gritty. The search has to make its way through the complications of each of our lives, through the ephemeral appearance (we who are Christians believe) of God incarnate as Jesus Christ and also through the rubble in Port-au-Prince where so many lives were meaninglessly, horribly crushed in an instant—mothers and fathers, brothers and sisters, innocent children.

Faith that can't withstand getting rocked by all of this ought to crumble like those concrete buildings. But faith that isn't shaken regularly by life isn't trustworthy either. Maybe this crisis of faith, this search for faith is something like yours.

I'm a Christian trying to be as faithful as I can. But some days I'm a determined agnostic. Other days I'm just indifferent and making it through life's ups, downs and "to do" lists in such a way that whether God exists doesn't seem to matter. Sometimes I believe in God but would rather not consent. I'm conservative some days, wishy-washy on others. Through all the iterations, I've returned to find God—specifically in Jesus—inviting me into love and gratitude.

But with each shock and aftershock in life—and this earthquake was one of them—the search seems to restart. Then I see whether I keep finding faith or not in the middle of the suffering and uncertainty of this world.

PART ONE

Confronting
a Crisis of Faith

FAITH CAN SEEM CERTAIN. A sense of peace or clarity, the mysterious beauty of life, or the transformations seen in yourself, in someone else, in a community—it couldn't be other than God.

But there are also shocks to the system when God seems either absent or negligent. Do we ignore these shocks and their aftershocks?

Sometimes a crisis of faith happens in an instant; other times it's a drift into uncertainty.

Welcome confirmations of faith. And just as important, pay attention to the crises of doubt or unanswered questions. Honest faith doesn't deny God, but it doesn't deny the uncertain and painful reality of life either.

1

THE WORLD
CRASHES ALL
THE TIME

How long, O Lord?

PSALM 13:1

Living in this world means it might crash down on you at any moment. We're vulnerable. It can happen emotionally or physically, economically or spiritually. It can happen to us or to someone we love. It can happen to me, which I don't like. It can happen to my young daughter or son, which I hate.

And God is responsible—or to put it another way, *to blame*. The more theologically correct formulation is that God created what was good, love required a certain freedom, and we made/make a mess of it. I kind of believe that. But it's also clear from our daily reality— even confessing the suffering, resurrection and hope of Christ—that we've been set loose in a deeply flawed system.

It's not that I'm ungrateful. I recognize God is *to blame* for every good thing too. But sometimes suffering eclipses the good. The earthquake of Port-au-Prince was among the world's most dramatic crashes of the past hundred years. Less dramatic crashes happen too, all around us: People in our church in Florida have lost their jobs and homes in the past year. Children die in car accidents. Friends are diagnosed with cancer. A tornado tears through my sister-in-law's town. Fractured relationships and disappointments surround.

In response to these crashes, I've been in a cold war with God, setting up a demilitarized zone between God and me, like between North and South Korea. There are occasional diplomatic excursions (over bread and wine) or small flare-ups (angry prayers), but too often my strategy is silence and avoidance. And as these things tend to go, the main result of my brilliant approach is that I feel my soul/spirit/heart atrophying.

There has to be a better way. The psalmists somehow got away with celebrating the God who is, while sneaking in cries for a different God than the one we have, one whose justice is more active, who is more present, who takes our frailty more compassionately into account. They praised God for loving everyone, but then sang about revenge fantasies of smashing babies against rocks. The Psalms aren't a self-help manual that smoothes out the edges and navigates clearly through uncertainty. Rather, I find the Psalms uniquely honest as they are in turn faithful or doubt-riddled, cringe-inducing or exuberantly worshipful, polished or raw, holy or irreverent.

In short, they're alive.

So how to make our way through the rubble in this crash-prone world without becoming bitter or indifferent—or being willfully blind to reality as a way to cope? In short, how can we be alive with honest faith?

I realize I'm losing this cold war. The space between God and me (which, in faith, we call a soul) feels at the moment like a barren, dusty, no-man's land. I want the life I see in the Psalms. How can I find it amidst the rubble and dust? At minimum, how do I make this cold war hot, which would at least be a sign of life? It seems a soda vendor named Blaise might help—Blaise and my friend Enel, who found himself suddenly under the collapsed concrete in Haiti.

◆ ◆ ◆

On January 12, 2010, Enel is working in our office just off Rue Delmas, a main street of Port-au-Prince that runs up the middle of the city, past the boys who rub your windshield with a dirty rag for change, past a couple of grocery stores for the small middle- and upper-class, past the gas stations, and ends where it forks on either side of the Petionville cemetery.

He leaves the office, walks up the street a block and climbs the stairs to the third floor of a six-floor university building for an afternoon class on pedagogy. The professor is late, so Enel goes to the back to talk with a couple of friends about missed homework. Twenty-five classmates chat and wait.

The building starts to shake. Then more violently.

Enel grabs the iron bars over the open window beside him.

Shaking and shaking, stronger and stronger.

The building comes crashing down with all of them inside. The crunching of collapsing concrete. The screams.

Enel grasps the window bars as he falls.

A large slab of concrete—one of the walls or a section of ceiling—smashes into his back, but then likely saves his life as he lays shielded under it.

Three more stories come crashing down.

The two friends he was talking with are also alive. They each dig themselves out in about fifteen minutes and then scatter, as they're able, to find loved ones. Crushed classmates are strewn nearby. Others are unseen, buried. Cries of *"Amway!"* Help! come from different directions in the rubble.

Enel can barely walk. At first he thinks only their building fell. A stranger is walking down the street through the dust and past the car smashed under a collapsed wall. He puts an arm around Enel to help him limp two blocks to the place where he'd normally catch a bus toward his home outside the city. At the corner they pass a girl with her hand reaching out through the concrete, calling out, *"Sove m! Sove m!"* Save me! Save me! and he can only limp by. He realizes as they go that it's not just his building, or his block, or that neighborhood. Something vast has happened.

A fault line jolts a wide, jagged line of victims simultaneously. A tsunami crashes in along the shore, hits in an instant all in its path. But consciousness of horror like this spreads more like concentric waves moving out from a pebble—or gigantic boulder—dropped in a lake.

Enel arrives at an intersection normally jostling with vehicles and pedestrians. Now it's filling with people who are stunned and injured, people who are lying streetside, some with crushed limbs, some newly dead. Enel sits, then lies down. He realizes he can't get up. His adrenaline reserves are spent.

Enel's face (like in those eerie, early pictures) is covered with fine concrete dust from the collapsed school, from the dust that rose after a city of two million people was shaken like an old rug.

And he is thirsty. So thirsty. Dusk is settling in. He doesn't think he will make it through the night because his mouth and throat are caked with dust. It feels hard to breathe. Soon after he thinks about this, a different stranger walking by pauses, holds a four-ounce bag of treated drinking water, pours some to gently wipe the caked dust off Enel's face, then gives him the rest of the water to drink. The stranger continues on his way.

Night is arriving. Hundreds of people assemble in the public square where Enel is lying, because their homes have collapsed or are unsafe. Just across the intersection, a mutual friend and colleague of mine and Enel's, Guilloteau, is also spending the night in the square with his wife and young son, Max. Guilloteau had been in his church, which didn't collapse. An elementary school across the street did. Guilloteau and others immediately started helping to pull children out of the school.

In the middle of helping, Guilloteau suddenly thought of his wife and young son. He took off sprinting through the city's devastated streets, past more people crying out for help, running many blocks in his dress shoes. He found his family outside their apartment. They were safe, but the apartment walls were fissured and it was no longer livable.

In the dark there were aftershocks and fear. What was it like spending the night lying in that square with hundreds of people, unable to move? What sounds mingled with the dust in the air? Cries of agony? Silence in the face of such disaster? Moans of those in pain? Hushed conversations as people who were able tried to comfort each other?

"No," Enel says. "All night long we were singing and praying to God."

They sang church hymns together. Other times people improvised their own hymns in response to what they'd just survived. And they prayed.

Angry prayers? Questioning prayers?

No, mostly prayers of gratitude because we were spared, Enel tells me, and prayers for those who weren't. All night long.

An evening of suffering and faith passed in that square and city that was worthy of being recorded in the book of Acts. It doesn't seem an exaggeration to say Enel took part in one of the more remarkable nights of faith in the world's history.

Is it staying true to the raw emotional honesty of the Psalms to wonder whether God was worthy of the incredible response of faith and worship that night?

♦ ♦ ♦

Three weeks after the earthquake, Enel and I are both amazed he's alive as we step through the sharp smell of decaying bodies coming up from under the rubble of his university. Rebars are twisted like flimsy spaghetti. Textbooks, emblems of a promising future, are strewn across the rubble, unclaimed by either the dead or the narrowly escaped. They're emblems now of crushed dreams.

We walk past a charred skull. Bodies that were close enough to the surface to find but too buried to extract had to be burned. Gasoline was poured down the cracks and lit with a match.

Leaving the university rubble, we walk half a block down the road where a crew of people wearing matching T-shirts is each being paid about six dollars a day to clear roads and sidewalks. A fridge is turned on its side with a block of ice and sodas and water inside.

We stop for a drink. Scrawled across the side of the fridge are the words, "God Is Verry Good." The double r is maybe a sign of emphasis or wavering, or simply a misspelling.

The drink vendor is named Blaise. We buy our drinks and start talking with him. Standard questions: "How's your family?" Profound sadness is conveyed mathematically these days—number of family alive/dead and homes collapsed or not.

"Where were you when the earthquake hit?" I ask.

Blaise is an intense guy. A little skittish but looks me straight in the eye.

"I was sitting over there, across the street. In a shady spot."

"What were you doing?"

"Reading my Bible," he says in roughly the same way Clint Eastwood's character in a Western would say, "Cleaning my gun."

"What were you reading?"

"Matthew 24."

He's not the first person to tell me this is what he was doing during the earthquake. In the second verse of the chapter Jesus says ominously, "Truly I tell you, not one stone will be left here upon another; all will be thrown down." It's about the temple being destroyed, about earthquakes and other signs of end times. Jesus is painting a vivid, awful vision of the future. The point is to persevere in faith and be vigilant about the truth. The final hour is unknown and will surprise many. I doubt Blaise was actually reading that chapter from Matthew's Gospel at the moment the quake struck. It's possible, but my better guess is he's trying to make sense of the insensible. I want to know more.

"Your cooler says, 'God is very good.' You still believe this?" The scent of death at the university is a hundred feet away. If this question can't be asked here, now, then we ought to stop asking it.

The Psalms suddenly incarnate. The passion of that roughly 2,500-year-old collection of poems comes to life as Blaise steps closer to me, now speaking faster in Creole with English peppered in. He's talking about how good God is, but in a way that's angry, electric. Because his faith is so alive, I keep asking more. He eagerly keeps talking, but eventually it becomes clear that if I push much harder—if I keep asking questions about God—I might get punched in the mouth.

Not because of his doubts or because he's protecting something fragile, though. He doesn't have a self-serving agenda or cheap certainty, like those blabbering on American TV and in too many public offices (and pulpits?).

It's the opposite of all this. It's fragile because it's so real. He's hurt. Maybe I can say it this way: it seems the guy truly loves God but is profoundly hurt that God would allow the suffering all around him.

It's like they're in an intense lovers' fight that I'd best not get in the middle of. We say goodbye.

◆ ◆ ◆

The way Blaise was confronting God (and me about God) brings up one of my character flaws, which is that I usually avoid confrontation. Dealing with conflict is not my forte. When the topic came up in a premarital counseling session, the counselor pointed out (after some probing) that it could be because my parents never fought in front of us and to my knowledge hardly ever disagreed. (Parenting: You can't win, can you?)

I have friends who regret saying things hot-headedly that they shouldn't have. I more often regret not saying things I should have. Like when I was walking through the Disney World parking lot to the trolley to meet my family, who had already arrived with my parents-in-law. Beside me was a father humiliating his ten-year-old daughter, saying, "You're useless! Good for nothing!" as the mother looked ashamed and stayed silent like the rest of us.

The kid's spirit seemed to leave a thin, splattering trail of blood behind on the pavement as she slouched into the Magic Kingdom, where dreams come true. I didn't say anything to this dad, honoring the fact that they were family . . . though he wasn't honoring it. In my little way I felt shame for not saying anything. The mom must live with incredible shame for not standing up, whether she herself is broken or in a deep malaise.

To avoid confrontation with God, sometimes I try to numb my life with too much sleep or a lack thereof, with too much work, with music, with absorption in relationships, or with avoiding relationships because they make you even more lonely if you're not being authentic.

But to avoid suffering and disappointment means to avoid life itself.

So I'm left knowing this: being authentic—naked and honest—before God feels like a matter of life and death. With so much at stake, it can only hurt to leave our real questions and protests unvoiced.

It's normal after a tragedy, whether widespread or personal, to ask privately and sometimes publicly, "Where was God? Can I still believe in God?"

I was asked this often after the earthquake, by people who know my connections to Haiti (three schools we work with collapsed, though nobody died or was injured). It's a fair question. But the earthquake revealed nothing new. The tragic, indifferent, brutal nature of life was already plainly evident. The way poor people are even more vulnerable than the relatively wealthy was already plainly evident.

If one of my children were diagnosed with a fatal disease, it would reveal nothing new about the world or God. I shuddered while typing that. Friends are going through this now; the most awful things imaginable already happen all the time.

For those who live by some faith, who want that faith to be eyes-wide-open honest, who want to be able to respond to goodness with gratitude, isn't life itself a kind of continuous crisis of faith?

SO GREAT

My friend Jon Paul and I were studying religion and history in India during a monsoon summer. We spent time at a Christian seminary and visited Hindu temples, Muslim mosques, Jain and Buddhist sites. I read novels by Salman Rushdie and others during interminable train rides (like the one from the southwest of the country up to Delhi that took sixty-seven hours; I still remember the surreal purple hue of the cabin).

One of our visits was to a Christian-run orphanage for children with severe physical and mental disabilities.

The staff was caring. The facilities were clean but resources obviously spare. We were introduced and, as often happened when we visited different schools, children sang a song. Like in Haiti, this is part of the culture. Often Jon Paul and I were invited to reciprocate. At one school we had done an impromptu "Amazing Grace" duet. We sang "Blowin' in the Wind" at a celebration of India's fiftieth anniversary of independence (don't ask; still hard to understand how this happened). Other times we did solos. Jon Paul had done the most recent solo for us elsewhere, so it was my turn in the orphanage.

I stood up in front of these forty severely disabled children and start singing the only children's song with actions that came to mind:

My God is so big,
so strong and so mighty
There's nothing my God cannot do.
The mountains are His,
The oceans are His,
The stars are His handiwork too.

I was doing the actions. The words came out of my mouth, each instantly sinking like a ton of theological bricks. A teacher next to me copied my actions—holding her arms out for God's grandeur, flexing her biceps to show God's strength. Meanwhile, because of their disabilities, only a few of the children had the God-given capacity to do even these most simple of motions about God's goodness and omnipotence.

My God is so big,
so strong and so mighty
There's nothing my God cannot do.

It's like Christopher Hitchens and Richard Dawkins cowrote *Atheism: The Musical* and I unwittingly became the star.

On that day the solo couldn't end quickly enough for me. That I can't sing well was by far the least of the problems. I could blame only my faith and song choice. And yet with those children is precisely the place to search for whether or not it's possible to sing, and what the lyrics should be.

2

SPIRITUAL AFTERSHOCKS

Will you forget me forever?

PSALM 13:1

We're each in our respective beds for about fifteen minutes when the little tin house we're in starts to shake. It quickly gets loud from the rattling of the roof sheeting that now makes up both the roof and the walls. After a few seconds I swing my leg over the side of the bed to stand up on the floor, which is left over from the concrete block home that crumbled a few weeks ago. Enel sits up. Guilloteau starts toward the door.

An aftershock.

Then it's over. It wasn't violent. Nothing fell. It wasn't frightening, except as a reminder of what had happened. The three of us soon start laughing the laughter of relief as we wonder why Enel, who had tumbled three stories before, had not immediately bolted out the door.

We were in Woshdlo (near Darbonne/Leogane), staying in the

remainder of the house where my wife and I had lived with a Haitian family for our first seven months in Haiti. We learned the language and culture from them. Through the (at times, bumpy) experience we became like family to each other and have stayed close for the past eight years. One of the grandchildren is now our goddaughter.

During the first few days after the earthquake, we didn't know if any of them were seriously hurt, if they were alive. They live near the epicenter. Phones were down in the country. Then four days after the earthquake, our phone rang just after midnight.

It was them. We talked for nine minutes before we got cut off. The family in Woshdlo was unharmed. The three small family homes, however, were destroyed, including the house we'd lived in. "You'd get lost if you tried to find us here, with all that happened in the town," they told us. An older woman I bought bottled water from in town during each visit died under her home. As the names flew by too fast over the iffy phone connection, I didn't recognize all of them. Most of the people named were alive; some were dead.

This visit with Enel and Guilloteau was my second one with the Woshdlo family since the earthquake. My first post-earthquake visit with them had been six days after the disaster. When I arrived, the kids had shown me where the family was sleeping: on the ground among the dried beanstalks, under a tarp and some sheets supported by four sticks. Their neighbor Frefre, also a good friend of mine, was there. I asked where he was staying, since I'd walked past his destroyed house next to the path. He pointed twenty feet away to the makeshift tent of bed sheets supported by four sticks. His sheet was bigger than the Woshdlo family's, and his sticks were about five feet tall instead of only three. They had already told a few jokes, so I said, "Oh, you're in the bourgeois place?" They all laughed.

In the days following, they—like anyone who could—got to work making shelters with what was available, in this case wood beams and tin-roof sheets. In addition to being available, these materials wouldn't kill anyone if the shelter collapsed on them while they slept.

Wherever I was with Enel in Port-au-Prince, say, visiting a colleague, his eyes would scan the building right away when we got inside. The first time I didn't understand and asked if he was okay. He kept looking around and then said, "If it starts to shake and we jump behind that tree, the way the wall will fall, I think we'll be okay."

Another aftershock. This one in Enel, in how he sees buildings and walls. How can this new habit of his not last a lifetime?

I think of my own spiritual aftershocks, which I have sometimes when I'm alone and other times in conversations like this back in the United States:

"Did you see the news today?" someone asks me. "A woman was pulled from the rubble, fourteen days later, still alive!"

"Wow, that's amazing," I say.

"And she came out singing a hymn and praising God. What a testimony."

"Yeah, people's faith there is really incredible. I'm humbled by it all the time."

"And what an amazing miracle, isn't it? God is good."

We grope at straws trying to make sense of the suffering. To fill the silence, we say things that are sincere but sometimes silly. We find slivers of Scripture that prop up our defense, but do we want the kind of God that the logic of our straw-patched statements creates?

"What a miracle how that girl was pulled from the rubble!"

The straw God spoke into being by this statement is one whose power and compassion are disturbingly out of whack. If God could orchestrate the rescue of the one, then why wouldn't God have protected the many in the first place? Little Mike gets diagnosed with leukemia and evacuated within hours—but from a city in ruins. Friends told me about an eight-year-old girl who survived when the building she was in collapsed—but her mom and sister died in front of her, and her father had died some years ago. She wandered the streets in shock. Days later someone found her and got her back to her village. At that point do you say, "What a miracle of God that she survived and was brought back to her village!"? Isn't that like a babysitter taking your three children out for a canoe ride, returning with only one—because the other two drowned—and then expecting to be congratulated for bringing back one of the three alive?

"Well, people down there have always been really poor, right?" Or *"They believe in voodoo, right?"*

Most people avoid saying these types of statements (one prominent TV personality aside) because when said aloud the monstrous logic is so clear. But I have heard them spoken in conversations, and they often seem to linger in the background as a way to find some order. The logic implied is that God's rain falls on the just and unjust, but God's judgment is highly selective and tends to fall especially hard on those who are poor (and whose skin isn't white). But what about my friend Emmanual? He is a pastor and a motorcycle taxi driver (who drove my wife and me to the sonogram appointment where we confirmed that Shelly was pregnant with our daughter). When the earthquake struck, he was out working on his motorcycle. Hundreds of people in his church (including two of his sisters and a brother) were together at a prayer service in the name of Christ. They were all killed. God, then, must not judge only harshly—at least that would be consistent—but also capriciously and disproportionately. The victims are to blame for the crime.

"At least they're in a better place now."

Even if we believe eternal life is true, which I do, that doesn't reduce present suffering, does it? And it's not a fair dismissal of suffering, because God put such value on this life. Nobody, not believer or atheist or anyone in between, is certain about whether there is a next life. Conceivably any suffering on earth could be eclipsed by the goodness of what is to come, but meanwhile a statement like this simply creates a monstrous God for whom the ends (even if they torture people) justify the means.

"Isn't it amazing that we [or a particular group of missionaries] happened to be there at just the right time to help?"

This self-help God provides suffering to some as an opportunity for others to express compassion or work on self-improvement. This wouldn't be an all-bad God if everyone made it through. Suffering *can* be positive for both the helpers and those being helped. But it's far from positive for everyone. Some die. Some suffer too much to ever recover. Others fail the opportunity for self-improvement and live lives of disappointment (often taken out on their own children). And doesn't this create a God who is a buffoon of a logistician—who can coordinate getting one group into the perfect place, but for some incompetence couldn't get the young mother off the porch before the concrete blocks collapsed on her?

"We might not understand, but it's all part of God's plan." Or *"It was meant to be."*

Wouldn't any plan this flawed be sent back for major revisions before it could be put into place? The architect says, "Here's the building design, but occasionally the elevator will malfunction and a dozen or so people will plummet to death.

The water piped in for the daycare is occasionally radioactive and will cause slow, painful deaths for some of the children. Oh, and the entire building will collapse in the middle of the business day every few years, but we'll rebuild." Um, back to the drawing board please. This platitude about God's plan is often said citing the verse in Romans 8:28 that "all things work together for good"—but surely the assertion of faith is that "in all things God works for the good of those who love God," that God eventually overcomes evil with good, not that all this madness is part of a detailed plan.

But without these simplifications, what can we say to fill the heavy silence? The simple answers are all unsatisfying as attempts to settle the aftershocks of suffering. Hopefully, in faith and doubt, part of faithfulness is to keep asking, listening and asking again. I'm searching for what to say instead.

Spiritual aftershocks aren't bad. Admitting and paying attention to them can lead toward an honest faith. Questioning God seems like a way to shatter the false, straw gods—or at least the distorted God—who otherwise leave me an atheist.

Oversimplifying God and suffering is not the only silence-filling tactic though. Sometimes our tendency is to avoid the conflict—to refuse to question God at all—by obscuring the discussion. Some philosophers and theologians say "judging God" is misguided because we're evaluating God as a moral actor within the world by human standards, though actually God is ontologically different. But as we're left reeling by suffering, I don't buy that we can't—acknowledging our mortal perspective—question God according to God's own given standards of love. (Okay, there is a philosophical conundrum in that previous sentence, but I'm sticking with it.)

The discussion can also be obscured by reverence. Some, so certain in their faith and understanding of these things, say you shouldn't question God. I think many of them are sincere. It's the ones who are certain without humility—and very publicly—that I find most disturbing. Aren't those who would protest most vociferously against revealing the agnostic chinks in their personal faith-armor trying, as Bono sings, to help "God across the road like a little old lady"?

Are those who assert it's self-evidently provable that God exists, that they know God's mind, DNA, design and playbook—are they like those pastors and leaders who are most anti-gay/lesbian but who then get caught with their same-sex lovers or masseuses or whatever their excuses? Are those who never confess that it might not all be true (especially with all the intricate scaffolding they've built up around God) really the ones with the least faith of all, the ones scared that their God will tumble before feeble puffs of doubt from mere mortals?

The net effect of either saying "God's goodness is unquestionable and always evident" or "God transcends discussions of good and evil" is the same: avoidance and untended doubt.

But maybe I'm just jealous that God has been revealed to them more clearly than to me (and this knowledge is grace, right? So you're not supposed to be able to lord your certainty over others as self-righteousness?). My faith feels helpless at times, like Isaac tied up on the altar, unsure whether it will survive. Will my faith in God die at the latest dagger drawn or be unbound and given new life? Or will it be released but then no longer want to trust the God who has been newly revealed?

♦ ♦ ♦

The day after the nighttime aftershocks in the little tin-roof house, we visited another friend in town. Their house was damaged but nobody had died. And though they were sleeping outside, during the day they used the concrete house. (Reasoning: you'd be fast enough to get out in time when awake, not while asleep.) We sat on the porch talking . . . and then some shaking started. Following their lead, I stepped quickly off the porch into the front yard as we kept talking.

Meanwhile, as soon as the earth started shaking, neighbor kids who were playing out in the next yard began jumping up and down cheering it. Fists pumping in the air. Whooping it up like their favorite team just scored a World Cup goal.

It was a dissonant scene in the midst of it all. It was defiant joy: a kind of "Mock the devil that he may flee from you." Or "You've stolen everything we have, including all our tears, but you can't get our laughter." Or just kids being kids.

The monstrous gods we create in response to suffering leave me an atheist at times. I wonder if I'm not an atheist—or at least agnostic—sometimes even with the true God. But maybe those kids (the more I thought about it, the more striking those resilient, defiant kids were) show a way to respond to my spiritual aftershocks.

Those kids don't cower or pretend the shaking isn't happening. They know it's dangerous, but they're alive, and after each aftershock they let God and the tectonic plates know exactly how alive they still are.

An Annotated Wish List
for Changes in/by God

1. Rather than a God of occasional disaster-rescue miracles, I want a God whose miracles prevent the disasters in the first place.

2. Rather than a God who needed to retreat in order to leave room for human freedom and love, I want a God who finds a less painful way to make freedom and love work.

3. Rather than a system set up so that those who suffer most are also the most vulnerable (usually those who are poor), I want the wealthy to be the most vulnerable. An increase in money beyond one's necessity could inhibit the body's production of antibodies.

4. Rather than children being at the mercy of nature and of other people, I want no one to die or be physically or emotionally traumatized before turning twelve years old. Nobody. And the only ones who die between thirteen and eighteen should be those whose decisions represent a clear and present danger to others.

5. For every unethical action, there should be an equal and opposite reaction—immediately. If you inflict suffering, you should immediately suffer accordingly.

6. I want a small indicator button, like a low-battery light, on the prominent C7 vertebrae that protrudes slightly on the cervical spine at the base of the neck between the shoulders. A gentle red light would glow forty-eight hours before death is irreversible, when the downward spiral toward unconsciousness or pain has won. It would indicate time for final goodbyes with loved ones and that a final welcome from God is imminent: "You're released from this life. Welcome into the next one."

3

ACCEPT
UNCERTAINTY

How long will you hide your face from me?

PSALM 13:1

For a few weeks when I was in my early twenties I wouldn't let myself stand on the balcony because I thought I might jump.

I was staying with friends in the little town of Traiskirchen, Austria. The nearby tire factory dusted everything on the balcony and inside with black soot (little bits of rubber?), presumably including one's lungs.

A year out of college, I was working for a refugee ministry in Western Europe. I was sleeping on the living room floor. I was following the sinful saint through Frederick Buechner's *Book of Bebb* novels. At the nearby ice cream store, I flirted with a cute server as best I could in broken English and German *("Ein eis bitte")*.

My job was interesting and meaningful. I was lonely at times, but not unusually so. Yet during those few weeks, I had to forbid myself from going out on the balcony when I was alone.

The discomfort was uncertainty. The tempter was, well, certainty.

I wasn't in acute psychic pain or heavy depression. I just wanted to know. I *needed* to know. (I also remember at that time desperately wanting to be "understood," so maybe they're related, the need to know and be known.) It's hard not to laugh a little at myself with the vastness of what I wanted clear, certain answers to:

What is true?

Does life go on after death—and if so, on precisely what basis will we be judged?

Really, how can sexual intimacy be reserved for marriage, which in our culture does not usually happen till well into our twenties or thirties, and masturbation not be biblically encouraged? (Okay, this wasn't one of the existential questions, but there was a very fit couple in the apartment across the square from the balcony whose athletic, silhouetted lovemaking was hard to miss some evenings.)

God, are you there? I need to know.

Jumping would have been misguided, but I was longing for God, for love, for assurances. I miss that sense of longing these days; for all its desperation, there was a purity to it that is missing in the cold-war distance I feel lately—the occasional détente notwithstanding.

David Hart, in his book *The Doors of the Sea: Where Was God in the Tsunami?*, communicates the prevailing logic of faith in the face of the inexplicable that makes sense to me but must drive nonbelievers crazy:

> Every free movement of the will is possible only by virtue of the more primordial longings of all things for the beauty of God . . . and so every free act—even the act of hating God— arises from and is sustained by a more original love of God. It

is impossible to desire anything without implicitly desiring the infinite source of all things; even the desire of suicide for the peace of oblivion is born of a love of self—however tragically distorted it has become—that is itself born of a deeper love for the God from whom the self comes and to whom the self is called.

Back on that balcony I had a crisis of uncertainty that pointed to this deeper love and faith. More recently I've tried to avoid such intensity, in part because life, family and work get increasingly busy. But to put my spin on Hart's passage, the way to seek God's love is with dedication and intensity—whether in love or in protest—because this at least keeps us in touch with our Creator. Avoiding intensity and potential crises of faith while hoping they might go away is not the way of Christ.

Blessed are those who touch and feel and believe—responded the resurrected Jesus to his doubting disciple, Thomas—but even more so, blessed are those who can't touch and feel but still believe. This is a startling (if heartening) admission by Jesus about the difficulty of what he's left to us, maybe in our time more than ever before. Up on that balcony, I wanted to touch the truth. A lifetime of uncertainty seemed like too much. I wanted to put my fingers into Jesus' side. To eat fish with him on the beach.

But we don't get to touch him . . . even as yet the pain touches us and those around us so forcefully. The whisper-touch of grace is usually so much lighter than the gale of pain. That's the nature of our crisis: God begs us to take hold of a (uncertain) whisper, all the while demanding that we let go of pain that has us firmly (certainly) in its grip. It doesn't make sense, and I need to figure out sooner rather than later what to keep believing.

◆ ◆ ◆

My buddy Owen has a long, storied dating history that goes back, in my memory, to when we were in eleventh grade and he dated _____, a girl in our class. I had a crush on her. Owen dated her. Yes, I was jealous of him both specifically about her and generally that he knew how to date. At that point I hadn't yet broken through being timid to start being awkward.

Through our years of friendship, I haven't always been the best help to Owen. When we were attending the same graduate school, for example, after talking one night about a fellow student he liked as we had a couple of beers at the local pub, I advised that his buzzing 1 a.m. lucidity would certainly break through her reluctance to start spending more time together. When we got to her door, Owen started questioning whether this was really the best strategy. So I quickly knocked and, like a junior high brat, ran down the hall and down the stairs back to my dorm room. I don't recall that she was impressed.

We who are Owen's friends of course hope he'll soon find the right woman to marry, but meanwhile we get to vicariously live his adventures in dating. (My wife and I both work and have two young kids. It's hard to remember dating; we barely manage foreplay.) His relationships tend to follow a familiar pattern that, strangely, makes me wonder about my relationship with God:

Stages of a Doomed Relationship

1. Owen starts dating someone. (The most entertaining stories come from this stage.)

2. Hope and first kisses and evangelical fervor.

3. Eventually he starts talking about the woman in a way that makes clear to the listener that they're not compatible.

4. He continues to date her but starts wavering based on the

increasingly obvious fact that the relationship won't work.

5. Both Owen and his girlfriend experience increasing levels of distress as they barrel toward the inevitable (okay, he tells good stories at this stage too, but you feel a little guilty about their entertainment).

6. They break up.

7. They relapse a few times.

8. After emotional misery is maximized for everyone involved, they end things firmly and finally.

Owen's cycle isn't unique. Most of us have lived something like this, whether in teenage infatuation or more seriously in a strained marriage. But here's the thing: after watching the added pain for Owen of having to cycle through these last stages, if my relationship with God is going to end with breaking up, I want the inevitable to happen now, not later.

If I'm not going to believe in God because an earthquake or tsunami can bring the world (whether concrete or water) crashing down on so many indiscriminately, then I don't want to believe in God now.

If I'm not going to believe in God in sickness, then I don't want to in health.

If not when worse, then I don't want to when better.

If I'm not going to believe in God after I lose a child, then I'd rather the break-up take place right now and not give allegiance in the meantime.

God, I'm sure, deserves a relationship that is far less fickle, and I think I deserve (or at least long for) a relationship that is far more evident.

But I don't want the relationship to drag out if it's doomed already by the reality that is to come.

◆ ◆ ◆

Many people, when God's goodness comes into question, think of God in one of two ways:

1. *The Benefit-of-the-Doubt God*

This is the God presumed by pop culture and promised, in its worst form, by the prosperity gospel. Professed by proof-texting and a secret belief in positive-only karma, this God wants wealth and goodness and happy endings. Essentially, God is the director of life's romantic comedy—inserting plot conflict to keep it interesting and to give characters opportunity for personal growth, but pulling strings so the ending is ultimately redemptive in this life.

When the plot goes really wrong, then it's our fault, not God's; we don't believe enough or aren't good enough. If we find we can't blame ourselves, we console ourselves that it's only a movie; the divine reality is yet to come. Hope and faith come at the cost of truth.

There are of course other, better versions of this. Actually, most of the devout Haitians I know think this way, even after the earthquake. The friends I talked with about these questions were still in worship, still devout, seeing the earthquake as a problem of nature and not a problem of God.

2. *The Guilty-till-Proven-Innocent God*

This approach says God is on trial for the sufferings of this world—and the verdict is not promising. Goodness and beauty do not balance out the horrors. Or at the very least it's a draw. Those who view God this way consider benefit-of-the-doubt believers naive. What kind of good Creator could possibly survive when 230,001 people don't survive under the created order (and human-created conditions) that just crashed on them?

One of novelist Dostoyevsky's characters in *The Brothers Kara-*

mazov doesn't shy away from putting God on trial. He famously details the suffering of a boy and girl and concludes that he will respectfully return his ticket (to life) back to God—because even all the goodness of the world cannot be justified by the horrific suffering of one innocent child.

These two options aren't a rubric for understanding how everyone approaches the problem of evil-good. But when I vacillate, it's often between these two stances, which are both related to uncertainty. We have to (by faith, one way or another) try to make sense of so much good and so much evil—and what this says about God. All the cloud and dust of witnesses, the beauty and the cruelty of our world, the screaming and the singing, the glory and the horror of human experience must be called forth to testify.

While I was watching a basketball game the other night, an ad came on during a timeout. A montage of women's faces, one after the other, concluded with the statement, "A woman is sexually assaulted every two-and-a-half minutes." Then back to the game.

How do you go back to the game? Confronted with evil—an evil that will be repeated within two-and-a-half minutes, and then two-and-a-half minutes after that, multiple times before the next timeout. With any number of other evil acts and senseless suffering filling the seconds between assaults. Every moment, if we have eyes to see, presents another tangible reason for a crisis of faith.

At times, pain shapes us in good ways. We can't deny that. C. S. Lewis called it God's megaphone for getting our attention for our own good. But it can also crucify. And uncertainty in the face of it can leave us feeling paralyzed or stranded. It can make the leap of faith seem like a leap off the balcony of reality.

◆ ◆ ◆

I want the God of immediate, certain resurrection, but what we get now is the God of the cross.

This God embarrasses me a little with my four-year-old, who is fascinated by the Easter-story details.

"So, Daddy, how did Jesus die?" she asks, knowing the answer and yet wanting to hear it again. Of course she asks about the cross and not the rolled-away stone. (Just like she loved the story of the good Samaritan not for the neighborly love depicted but for the robber scene. Peace makes for good life, but conflict makes for good stories.)

"Jesus died on the cross," I say.

"How did they put him up there?"

"Well, by his hands and feet."

"But how?"

I keep it vague a few more times, but she knows, so I say, "They put nails in him."

I'm sweating. She's satisfied with her cross-examination. I love teaching her about Jesus, of course, but the scandal, which becomes tame and smooth in my mind, looks fresh and awful in its way as I listen through her young ears.

I feel like I should testify to the benefit-of-the-doubt God to her, even when I'm uncertain. But this contradicts the whole *honest faith* thing. (Alas, do I teach my children benefit-of-the-doubt faith until their teenage years, when the inevitable guilty-till-proven-innocent questions arise—at which point we can seek together?) The early work of churches is faith, baptism and confirmation, but then faith can be vulnerable to crumbling when the questions or life gets hard. Some leave church mostly confirmed in doubt as they discover their faith is without substance. (But maybe I'm just projecting my own faith problems onto churches and parenting.)

We're left to make a move of faith not toward a God who protects us from suffering with any consistency, but who instead suffers with us. The story of the cross says something undeniably true about suffering in the world; the move of faith is whether it also says something about God's love.

On the cross, Jesus expressed both ultimate faith and ultimate doubt, quoting Psalm 22: "My God, my God, why have you forsaken me?" And on the cross, the benefit-of-the-doubt God is nailed to the wood—as is the guilty-till-proven-innocent God. Both versions are on trial. The God of the cross isn't distant and does not shy from crises of faith.

We don't have to minimize either suffering or uncertainty. Our love for truth can help protect us from ourselves and from worshiping an untrue god that can't survive the trial of this world. Let our faith too be nailed regularly to the cross of this world. Any faith that dies there was dead to begin with. What is resurrected is Life.

CIRCLING LIKE ANGELS
(LIKE VULTURES)

On the plane with thirty-four people,
Circling in toward destruction.
Like angels (like vultures).
    Why?

The city collapsed six days ago. The easy-to-reach cadavers:
burned already.
The drive up Rue Delmas this time—the thousandth time—will
  apparently stink of rotting flesh instead of gas fumes.

    Why do we go?
    Flee in horror; run to watch.
    Run to help; flee to get away.

Many want to go help. More than can make it on the limited
flights. Waiting lines. Finding a way via the Dominican Republic.
Clamoring for access like it's a Disney ride in high season. It's a
small world, after all.

This time it makes sense for me. It didn't after the tsunami.
This time I have to go. I didn't after New Orleans.
I do now. (Celebrities always do. Good for them. They have the
means to do what makes them feel alive.)
My goddaughter is sleeping now in a bean field;
her family's home destroyed.

Death slammed shut for so many.
Peek-a-boo. Peek-a-boo. Open and shut. I just kissed my son
goodbye.

We circle in closer, like vultures, like angels.

I grew up on the edge of fundamentalism: Purity and Holiness,
words deeply important.
> Other words, to me, have taken higher priority now:
> Justice and Humility.
But the words change easier than the shape of your soul.

This drive for purity is in me and I recognize it now and am
disappointed that purity once again stays elusive, a shadow dancing
with blurry edges on the cave's wall as the real world operates
elsewhere.

And in this tragedy of historic proportions—not even purity here,
among the impure mix of shattered concrete blocks and blood?

No. Personally and in those I'm circling down with, one recog-
nizes the opportunity to help but also to be: courageous, heroic,
compassionate, and just a little better than everyone else who isn't
going. To feel more alive.

Some clamoring to get down are so transparent in their messages,
and on Facebook and on Twitter, doing it for their own sake. Can't
you invite admiration more subtly, I think in disgust? You'll blow
the cover for the rest of us.

Occasionally givers are mostly concerned about themselves, about
the integrity of their money, making sure it doesn't go to any
waste, making sure it goes to what they need to feel. Their attrac-
tion to help goes so quickly through the filter of their self-
importance that it's hard to take seriously.

Except that those in need seriously need them.

We each make meaning in our lives with our decisions.

This is what attracts us to suffering. The plot of our own stories makes more sense if we make a difference for other people.

We circle like vultures (like angels) seeking meaning, to reinforce the better parts of ourselves.

We're repelled but attracted to:

a. the genuine possibility of helping,

b. wanting the same help for ourselves if the roles were reversed, and

c. the possibility of finding meaning and feeling better about ourselves.

We want to help but are repelled when it:

a. brings us closer to meaninglessness, to questions rather than answers, and

b. reveals us as more selfish—even as we give—than generous.

We want to find proof of God, one way or the other.

We shouldn't turn away, one way or the other.

Like angels, we help. Like vultures, we scavenge on the suffering of others to feed our hunger for meaning. Purity cannot be checked in or carried on for these flights. The baggage is ourselves. Always ourselves.

The U.S. military radios approval to the pilot. Time to land. My heart isn't pure, but it is broken. I need to be near.

4

DON'T
TURN AWAY

How long must I bear pain in my soul?

PSALM 13:2

MY FRIEND LUKE WAS IN THE northern city of Cap-Haïtien when the earth shook. There was almost no damage in that area, which he'd moved to from the United States with his wife and three children six months earlier to work on education projects. He's also a professional photographer and filmmaker, so within thirty-six hours, as soon as he could find a ride, he left his family and got to Port-au-Prince.

Eventually he linked up with my friend John, who'd been in his home just outside Port-au-Prince when the quake hit. (This is the home Shelly and I built on land belonging to John and his wife, Merline, and that they've since expanded.) John had grabbed his two young children as he ran out of the house when it started shaking. If the home had collapsed, he would have been too slow getting out with them.

John and Luke made their way around the city in those early days after the earthquake. John was finding our colleagues and assessing how we could best respond as an organization. Luke was filming. The city was an open cemetery. They passed thousands of bodies in the roads. They passed garbage trucks overflowing with corpses. They passed piles of hundreds of bodies that had been lit on fire to dispose of them. Bodies. People. What do you call the remains of such horror?

About six weeks later Luke and I were talking just outside of Port-au-Prince. Luke has the skills of a professional and the heart-on-his-sleeve emotion of an artist. He'd done everything possible to get to Port-au-Prince. Now he was saying he wished he hadn't seen and experienced what he had. (I don't doubt he was telling the truth, though he would have regretted not coming too.)

As we talked he told me, "Someone sent us advice a few weeks after of what to do in emergency situations like this." The *Practices to Facilitate Responder Health and Well-Being* included tips like, "Discourage identification with the dead by not looking at faces and hands."

"Faces and hands seemed like all I looked at," Luke said.

His eyes had been pulled precisely to what made the dead individuals, not bodies. His heart led him correctly—but it was too much for his heart to bear.

You want to escape the awful suffering yet are pulled to concentrate on the hands and faces of the victims. You want to turn off the lead story on the local news but can't help hearing what went horribly wrong for someone. You want to get away from all the pain but watch the roster of criminal investigation TV shows—both fiction and documentary. You peek through clinched eyes at the replay of the quarterback's knee getting blown up by a defensive end. It's hard to turn from the gossip you hear on TV or from the neighbors or in the pews.

But if you actually do turn quietly away from serious suffering—of wars, of family, of a local family in need—that is uncomfortable too.

Once I was scheduled to attend a child's autopsy at the children's hospital in Toronto. The province's chief pediatric pathologist attended my parents' church. When I showed interest in his work, he invited me to come observe.

The appointment fell through. It was about ten years before I had children of my own. I'm glad I didn't see a child's body dissected. What was I thinking? For me, that would have stumbled over the line between not turning away from suffering and seeking it out in an unhelpful way.

(Incidentally, the doctor was later found to be negligent in his work, which had an impact on families and on criminal prosecutions surrounding the deaths of some of the children. Parents' worlds crashed down—first, the mysterious evil of SIDS, and then, in some cases, being wrongfully convicted of killing their own child, as if the loss of their baby wasn't enough.)

◆ ◆ ◆

Jesus couldn't avoid suffering; it sought him out. Once he and his friends were making their way to Jerusalem. It was a long walk. As they entered one of the villages along the way, ten men came toward them. Jesus' entourage was used to attracting increasing crowds, but I imagine there was something unnerving about the aggressive way this group was approaching. Suddenly the men stopped short.

"Jesus, Master, have mercy on us!" one of them called out.

A few seconds of silence and then they couldn't hold back as planned. Another man, and then soon all of them, started yelling "Have mercy on us!" again and again to make clear just how desperate they were.

Don't turn away, they were saying. Sometimes we're so damaged by wrongs done to us that all we can do is beg to be noticed.

Don't come near, they made clear by stopping short. Maybe too by

the way they shouted out their request. It was what they were supposed to do then as lepers as precaution against spreading the disease.
Sometimes, because we're so damaged, our only way to ask for mercy
or love is half-heartedly. We're protecting ourselves. We're protecting anyone who would help us: "This is so toxic—I need help but
you won't be safe if you're near me."

One of the skills of friendship and dating is keeping your raw
needs and hurts hidden from view so as not to scare the other person
away. You reveal them gradually to each other so they can be han-
dled. The lepers had neither the time (Jesus was just passing through)
nor any subtle options: the need and the distance were immediately
on display.

It's incredible how often people who could go in the opposite
direction *don't turn away*. Plenty do (including me, too many times to
count), but so often there is one or two who help. The miracle we
pray for, if we can pray, is for that person to come close enough. The
miracle we pray for, if we have enough courage, is for the courage to
go close to someone who is hurting deeply.

The lepers just stood there.

Don't turn away, and Jesus didn't. He healed them. He sent them
away for official full-health confirmation. He had met their challenge. Then he seems to have issued an unspoken "Don't turn away
from me" challenge of his own. And *he* waited.

Only one ex-leper came back, compelled by gratitude, and threw
himself at Jesus' feet, praising God in the same loud voice he had
initially used to ask for mercy.

Nine others didn't return. I'd always been taught that this was a
lesson about (a lack of) gratitude. One of the recent children's songs
being sung in our house jauntily makes this point.

But might the other nine have just been carried by joy? And who
could blame them for not losing any time getting to their loved ones

from whose embrace they'd been so cruelly exiled by disease? Jesus'
statement almost seems petty when the one leper comes back: "Were
not all ten cleansed? Where are the other nine?"

Isn't it enough, Jesus, that you set them free back to love? Isn't it
enough for you that they called out for mercy? Isn't the suffering itself enough for you? How much more can you ask? If you leave us at
a distance to suffer . . . can you then demand nearness and praise at
your feet when we're healed?

The God who we experience so often as distant will not settle for
us turning away from suffering—nor turning away from God. Or if
we do stay at a distance, it becomes our own loss.

This God demands nearness—and though, from my perspective,
Jesus' words to the one leper might seem petty, maybe he knows that
nearness is crucial for those he just healed. Is their healing incomplete
unless they intimately express gratitude? Does he want them to remember that they are connected to God both in suffering and healing?

Don't turn away because that makes it hard to really search for
God. If we turn away from suffering—and gratitude—we are left at
a distance from others, from ourselves, from God.

But it's hard to get close.

◆ ◆ ◆

Sara is a friend at church and an ER nurse. Her job is to deal with
suffering.

"I always want to be in a patient's room, no matter how bad the
suffering is. But it's so much better *when I know* the outcome will be
positive. When you know it's not going to work—especially with
kids—that's when it's really hard to be there.

"A year and a half ago, my first day back from maternity leave with
my daughter, a mom came in with her ten-day-old that she'd acci-
dentally rolled over on and smothered in her sleep. In a way I didn't

want to be in there, because it was so hard. It was clear the baby wasn't coming back. But I had to be in there. I just wanted to hold this mother, as a new mother myself. You know her life is never going to be the same. We were all crying—the nurses, the doctor, the cop.

"I don't cry during every shift, but, yes, I cry a lot. If you can't cry, I don't think you should be in this job. Otherwise sometimes people turn toward alcohol or drugs to cope. Or start to resent the patients."

Sara has found that each person has a different limit for being close to suffering—then they have to turn away. Recently a sexual-assault victim was recounting stories that were so intense, with sexual assault only part of it, that Sara had to go get another nurse to listen with her. It was too heavy to bear alone—even just in listening, *let alone experiencing.*

She says, "I make someone who is suffering feel better each day. That's amazing. I get to know them because it's so personal. They disrobe, they're naked, they're so at your mercy. You have to be so caring. They're so scared and looking to you for help while they're in front of you in a flimsy little green gown that's open at the back, as you poke them with sharp metal and give them drugs that, if you gave a wrong dose, could kill them.

"Sure, I struggle with God and why there is so much suffering—but have basically come to peace knowing I won't know till I'm with God after I'm dead. Faith and church make it possible for me to keep doing this.

"The greatest thing about the ER is you can have the entire human experience in a single night—from pure evil to this amazing goodness and love that surrounds many people. There's a quadriplegic who comes in regularly. The way her family takes care of her—her skin is amazing, for one, which takes so much attention from other people if you're a quadriplegic. Or you see an old couple and one spouse is really sick—and then see this incredible love and care. Love, even in all this, still usually overwhelms the suffering for me."

These appearances of love and compassion—and the ability to make a difference in the outcomes—make it easier to be close to suffering.

"I pray all through the night, as patients come in," Sara adds as she gets ready to start another all-night shift. "Sometimes I also find myself, halfway through the night, dropping f-bombs like crazy because of it all. Then I try to go have a little talk with myself in the corner."

◆ ◆ ◆

My friend Guilloteau often impresses me with how he faces suffering with integrity.

Even several months after the earthquake, after so much devastation and sleeping on the street, after sending his wife and child to live with other family so he could work, he was still deeply disturbed—almost ashamed—that he had stopped pulling children out of the collapsed school to run across the city and see if his family was okay. He brought it up a number of times. It's a faultless decision, but he felt like he'd turned away.

His willingness to face—and to try to help in—suffering was on display another afternoon, though, when he, Enel and I were driving from Port-au-Prince to visit a couple of our organization's schools in the countryside. Enel wanted to drive through the heart of downtown, which looked like it had gone through a five-year war in thirty seconds. Countless thousands of people had died in the densely populated blocks.

At one point I started to feel vulnerable down there. A lot of pedestrians and then a block with not many people. Roads blocked from rubble. Tough-looking young men. It always amazes me, when

I think about how much need there is in Haiti and what I might do if my family didn't have enough food, that it's not more dangerous—that people living on the edge don't turn more often to violence for survival.

So I was driving and feeling a little tense, and then I noticed Enel and Guilloteau get tense, which didn't put me more at ease. The men with T-shirts tied over their faces so they'd breathe in less concrete dust suddenly looked threatening.*

Finally we found our way out and onto a main street.

"That wasn't smart," Enel said.

Ten minutes later, as we were driving through another part of the city where violence occasionally flares up, Guilloteau said loudly, "Stop! I don't know what he's doing with her." Guilloteau then jumped out of the truck. Enel and I shrugged and watched as he walked across traffic to where a middle-aged man was leading a young woman by her shirt collar and yelling at her while menacingly carrying a long stick.

Many people were busily walking in the street but not noticing the man. Guilloteau went straight to step in front of him. In a calm way Guilloteau started talking with him. They went back and forth. Eventually others stopped and a crowd formed. The conversation got heated. Enel and I were a little nervous, though it was also easy to get philosophical and think this was the kind of intervention I might be willing to die in.

---

*It might have been briefly dangerous for us, but the situation in the city was awful for so many others. In postdisaster situations, some organizations come in and focus on protection of women and children, because they're vulnerable (to abuse, to rape, to theft) in chaos and because men can take advantage of the situation—and/or take out their own frustration and suffering on those who are weaker around them. Our organization partners on some projects with a courageous group of Haitian women, all victims of rape, who have banded together to work on victim care and on rape prevention. Some horrific things were happening in the tent camps in the months after the earthquake.

Finally Guilloteau started walking toward us. A crowd of at least fifty people was still engaged with the man. He jumped in the truck and said, "Let's go."

He explained that it was a father with his daughter. He'd disciplined her, she ran away from home, he went and found her and was now bringing her home to teach her a lesson. Guilloteau had slowed him down and the crowd was convincing him that beating her wasn't the right choice.

I was humbled to be Guilloteau's friend—that he would do that at any time, let alone at a time of suffering and survival. Conditions even much less extreme make many of us unable to look up and pay attention to the needs of others.

◆　◆　◆

Later that day, after we'd visited our schools, I was talking with a close friend under a mango tree. In another life, with fate meted out some other random way, she would be a nurse or a teacher, maybe a high-school principal. She's intelligent, playful and serious. I often ask her for advice on work or relationships in the community. She never had the chance to finish high school. She spends her days leaning over the cooking fire or the water basin scrubbing clothes.

I've always been impressed by her spirit. But when I was with her two months after the quake, she was in despair. She couldn't take it anymore. As we talked, her need felt to me, if I can say this without trivializing anything, as great as all that of Port-au-Prince—the need becoming personal and infinite. Just this one person whom I care deeply about.

Her spirit, much stronger than mine, had made the best of a hard life. But to lose her house, to see her community and her family lose so much, and then to face rebuilding her home and life in the midst of a devastated community where 90 percent of the homes were unlivable, with all the effort it would take just to get back to survival, it was too much. I glimpsed how this disaster had become part of her, had become an internal disaster too.

The depth of a person's suffering sometimes makes me turn away, whether in the United States or Haiti. With this friend, I wasn't attracted to or repelled by her suffering. I just listened. With what help I could offer, I didn't feel good about myself or feel guilty. I said goodbye feeling love and pain. Relationships and commitment protect against becoming a charitable angel or a descending vulture. I'd see her and her family again soon.

John, Luke, Sara, Guilloteau, Enel, Jesus, the lepers (all ten of them) and this friend each jerk my head and heart back around to where they should be: Don't turn away and pretend suffering isn't pandemic. Don't become a charitable tourist of suffering either. Pain is personal—with poverty and illness among the worst exacerbating factors—but also universal. Don't turn away from confronting my own cowardice. Don't turn away from doing everything possible to stop suffering. There's so much we can do nothing about, but we can help—sometimes one person and sometimes many.

We discover we're impotent and edge closer to despair; other times we become contributors to goodness and edge closer to hope. Whatever the outcome, not turning away seems vital to the work of trying to stay human, of trying to find truth, and maybe even God.

SURVIVOR'S GUILT

IF YOU'RE OVER THIRTY YEARS OLD and have relative health, regular food and secure shelter, how can you not feel some survivor's guilt in this world? (And if you don't, that's a problem too.)

Then there's posttraumatic stress disorder. This would presumably apply to a large percentage of those living in the Port-au-Prince area, though even this category must fall short in describing how people are affected by such a scale and depth of loss. Part of the definition in the *Diagnostic and Statistical Manual of Mental Disorders— Fourth Edition* (the standard guide on these things) is that a person faces a physical trauma (themselves or as witnesses) and that their response involves "intense fear, helplessness, or horror."

This is followed by the person reexperiencing the experience, avoiding associated stimuli, and having persistent new symptoms like problems sleeping or outbursts, which all last for more than a month and cause problems in social, occupational or other areas.

Not to minimize the extreme nature of what people in Haiti (or soldiers coming back from combat, for another example) are facing, but I'm struck by how, in a less acute way, this definition applies to almost everyone alive. Granted, some people can experience traumas and, through the difficulty, flourish. But others are crushed. Suffering becomes the sole arbiter of truth. And many of us, I think, are tempted to respond by walling off our hearts or ideals.

Recently I watched a bigthink.com interview with a psychology scholar named Tal Ben-Shahar, who taught the most popular class at Harvard. Some of his thoughts resonated with the Psalms and also with me intuitively:

There is a lot of research showing that the most successful people in the world, whether it's scientists or artists, are also the people who have failed the most times. It shows that ultimately the happiest people are actually people who allow themselves to experience the full gamut of human emotions, not people who suppress or somehow get rid of painful emotions when these arise. . . . You know, there are two kinds of people who don't experience painful emotions such as anxiety or disappointment, sadness, envy . . . the psychopaths and the dead. . . . The paradox is that when we give ourselves the permission to be human, the permission to experience the full gamut of human emotion, we open ourselves up to positive emotions as well.

Being shell-shocked by the traumas of life is a right response. Guilt is often a right response to being alive too, when we fail to love as generously as we should. But guilt and trauma shouldn't close us down. Being open to life is also the right response to life. It's what survivors should do as long as we can.

5

FEEL

How long must I . . . have sorrow in my heart all day long?

PSALM 13:2

When I was nine years old, our dog Kippy, a small black-and-beige mutt, died. We were out for a family bike ride one summer in Edmonton, Canada, where we lived, when Kippy dashed into traffic. Next he was breathing heavily in the back of our station wagon, his fur matted with blood. Then he stopped breathing. I don't remember crying when it happened, but I do remember crying hard into my pillow at night weeks later. It's the last time I remember really weeping.

Twenty-eight years later I don't seem to know how to cry, even though, like everyone, I've gone through plenty of experiences when it would have been appropriate. It's now built up to the point that I wonder—impossible to say this non-melodramatically—if I started crying, would I be able to stop? Am I unable to cry or somehow unwilling—and either way, what do I then miss out on? Is this an extension of my cold-war avoidance of God?

During that first trip to Haiti six days after the earthquake, I came as close to unbound weeping as I have since Kippy.

As I stood talking with friends next to their flimsy, makeshift shelters out in the bean fields, about thirty neighbors, most of whom I knew, came over. One of my friends pointed out a woman from the village holding her son. I didn't know her. She was wearing a red blouse and pink-flowered skirt. Her son, about five years old, had a white bandage wrapped around his head and a cast on his left leg. My friend said that her husband, the child's father, had died. I started talking with the mom.

She told me that she, her husband and their son were sitting on the front porch of the house when it started shaking. They scrambled to get out.

"So your husband grabbed your boy?" I asked.

"Yes," she said, as she held her son to her chest, his arms wrapped around her neck. "He grabbed him and held him *just like this,* like I'm holding him now, as he ran off the porch. But the concrete blocks collapsed and fell on them. My boy lived. My husband died."

Just like this and I choked up. *Just like this* as she held her son, the same way that I hold my daughter, who is about the same size. *Just like this* the child lost his father. *Just like this* the son fell with his father and his father's arms went limp.

Just like this the similarities between us opened a small window to the pain. I choked up and came close to completely breaking down. I would have been crying for the son and wife. Crying for the father, now gone. Crying for a country where this just happened, multiplied 230,001 times. Crying, yes, for myself.

It didn't seem the right time to weep in front of thirty neighbors who had lost so much. But I couldn't talk. It took ten or fifteen seconds to "recover." Damming up a waterfall of tears. My friend Jasper, the father of my goddaughter, was standing beside me. His own home collapsed two hundred feet away. He lost everything himself. His wife and two young children were out sleeping in a field. He put his arm around my back to comfort me.

Just like this if we're not turning away, then it seems we're turning toward tears—but hopefully also toward something else through the tears.

◆ ◆ ◆

My inability to cry feels like a deficiency. Recently I was telling my sister, who also works in international development (and has a Ph.D. in psychology), about my crying problem. She had just returned from doing work in Haiti after the earthquake. It was her second time there; her first visit was while Shelly and I were living in Haiti. She told me she'd broken down crying twice since returning, just thinking about the situation there, and then said, "If this work ever stops making me cry, then I'm going to quit."

Is my problem gender (boys don't cry), Freudian (my mom doesn't cry), something else—or not really a problem at all?

I called a professor who has researched crying at The Mood and Emotion Lab at the University of South Florida.* One of the lab's research aims is to replace myths about crying with scientific understanding. In this work they've found that people (and our culture) tend to remember crying as more beneficial than actually tracking it reveals crying to be.

(I just stopped writing and got up because my one-year-old son, Cormac, was crying in the next room; apparently a nap is not going to take. I'm not making this up for effect. I held him for a while, but he was crying as hard as he ever has and eventually let me know,

---

*The people in the lab deserve credit for the basic insights but aren't responsible for what I've done with them. The professor's study is serious and clinical, but I appropriate it in a personal way.

with outstretched arms, that only Mom would do at the moment. He's been sick for a few days, but it got worse today and he has a bodywide rash of little red dots. It's hard not to define the whole world by the sound of crying, so perfectly designed to unsettle those nearby, when it's going on around or in you.)

Still, crying can serve several important functions.

Crying can be cathartic (body, mind, soul). Feeling better afterward isn't just in our minds; there is a physiologically and emotionally satisfying release. Emotional tears aren't just salt water; they contain chemicals that differ from the tears released for lubrication from irritants (like onions or smoke). The hormones are prolactin, adrenocorticotropic (stress hormones) and leucine-enkephalin (a pain-reducing hormone), so research seems to show genuine emotional tears serve to flush out excess stress hormones.

Crying can be a signal—a plea for help or recognition. A child is born with this ability to signal; their lives depend on it. They learn how to use crying to call for help and attention (and, as any parent knows, to manipulate responses). And a baby's cry (as any parent also knows) is perfectly, gratingly designed to demand response. Maybe sometimes crying is a way for us to send God a signal as well: "SOS, your help is needed." Maybe some of us find that the help doesn't come, so we eventually stop trying. Crying can also be a signal to others—as well as to ourselves, whether we're an adult or a child—that something significant is happening. (Gustave falls, his tears fall, in the middle of the crowded street in the hour after the earthquake, when he spots the green-and-white uniform and then sees it's his daughter. Both catharsis and a signal that something incredible has just happened.)

Crying can overtake you. There's an almost mystical element to it that feels like something outside ourselves takes over and we lose some control. Crying can come unbidden. Maybe my desire to cry is a desire to be in contact with something outside myself, like the desire, as Paul writes in Romans 8, for the Spirit to step in to express what we most need through "sighs too deep for words."

I'm interested in sad tears—they are cathartic, a signal and a release of control. I want to get some of the sadness and hurt outside myself—and, conversely, to feel it more deeply, and without turning away.

In Psalm 42 the psalmist writes,

My soul is downcast within me. . . .
Deep calls to deep in the roar of your waterfalls;
all your waves and breakers have swept over me.
By day the LORD directs his love,
at night his song is with me—
a prayer to the God of my life. (TNIV)

I feel like missing tears means I'm missing out on a possibility for "deep to call to deep"—in this psalm like a waterfall. I want my sadness to know the sadness of God, and vice versa. Not that it will make it all okay, but I long for that connection. Right now my dry ducts and resentment feel like they keep me at a distance from God. So I read this psalm and want tears to wash me to the end where I can honestly say with the writer:

Why, my soul, are you downcast?
Why so disturbed within me?
Put your hope in God,
for I will yet praise him,
my Savior and my God.

God must be "the God of my life," quoting the first stanza—my whole life. But can I get to this praise without passing through the water of tears? I wish I could play the cello or sing gospel blues to connect from deep to deep. I don't feel myself still wanting to be understood (the flip side of that longing on the balcony some years ago). I think of it as an adolescent need that I'm past. But maybe that's not true.

In those days after the earthquake, I didn't sit and cry with Shelly. We prayed together and with our kids. We, of course, talked. But I should have cried with her so we could cry together. This is another failure of mine. There was lots of work to do, but there was time to cry.

So I put these words down, delete them, try again till I can get closer to what I think and feel and believe. This is my prayer, my confession. These words are my replacement tears, though they're not enough.

◆　◆　◆

One Easter before having kids, Shelly and I had friends over for dinner. Afterward the other husband and I went to rent a movie. We were both newly married and apparently still trying to impress our wives by getting a subtitled French film.

It was surely the most relentlessly sad movie ever made, I think, with parents dying and kids suffering and nothing improving one bit at the end. Which left us in the living room with two wives sobbing and two husbands silent. The movie ended and the only thing to do was mutter, "Happy Easter . . ." and say goodbye. It wasn't at-least-it-makes-you-appreciate-whatever-joy-you-can-find-in-this-moment sadness, but rather there-is-no-joy sadness.

We know that a limited amount of suffering or trauma can lead to a better life. It can form our character. It can shock us into refocusing on what is really important. It can break inertia and free us to find meaning and love in new ways. It can strengthen character and resolve, so our personal narrative becomes a story of perseverance and overcoming. The most beautiful, inspiring lives (and stories) overcome suffering—whether to gain self-control or to bring social change, to become virtuous where only damage had logical provenance.

But suffering can also break people. It can scar or debilitate too deeply to ever properly heal, so that the personal narrative becomes dominated by anguish.

The way the plot ends is the distinction between suffering and unbearable suffering, between meaning and meaninglessness. I want to be open to suffering so tears can flow and I can know something more about joy, but I don't want it to crush me.

I don't know how to both believe in the biblical story that culminates in Revelation with no more need for tears—and yet confess that the truth is now often closer to the French movie, as when 230,001 mothers, fathers, children, uncles, nieces die in an earthquake. A day of no more tears seems an eternity away indeed. There is nothing redemptive about that kind of loss. Of course good things have happened in Haiti since, but that kind of suffering and its aftermath still seem like crucifixion.

For Jesus' followers, Friday was the crucifixion, Saturday was the time of tears and uncertainty, Sunday was the resurrection. Faith confesses that the resurrection already happened. And yet it seems faith also leaves us in a perpetual Saturday—when the suffering (of people and thus of God) of the crucifixion stays just as near to us as the promise of resurrection. Sunday, we believe, is coming. But meanwhile, are we not left trying to live faithfully in this Saturday of Tears?

When Enel and I, with our friend Guilloteau, walked over the rubble of his six-story university three weeks after the earthquake, Enel was casual as he showed us where his classmates died and where he should have. He wasn't emotional at all.

Then we drove ten minutes to our friend Pastor Chassagne's

house. A tarp covered part of the yard where his family was sleeping. An older woman lay on a mat on the ground with her leg in a cast. As we got out of the truck, Pastor Chassagne, in his early sixties, who we'd normally greet with a handshake, came over and gave us each a big hug, saying, "I've lost so many. Now I have to give every friend a hug when I first see them. Every person who is still alive is a gift."

We met and talked about life and eventually work. Then about six of us sat in a circle to pray. After several of us had prayed, Enel started to . . . and soon into his prayer, just half an hour after walking over the rubble, he started weeping. His whole body shook and shook. This time I could be the one to put my hand on someone's back as Enel released what was inside, in catharsis, as a signal to God and us. He was still alive. He wept for a long time.

(My son wasn't well earlier today, as I mentioned, but he finally goes to sleep. We awake around midnight to his crying. Cormac can't catch his breath. Not wheezing or choking, just strange, shallow gulps for every attempt to breathe. I quickly drive him to the emergency room. Shelly calls our nurse friend, Sara, when I'm en route. She's on duty, so she takes us right back to a room. They give him oxygen through a little tube I hold up to his nose for half an hour. He's diagnosed with a respiratory virus. They give him simultaneous steroid shots in both thighs while he looks up at me in a moment of shock—why would I let them do that to him?—then wails for a couple of minutes. His breathing improves and I half sleep in the hospital bed curled around him, a monitor taped to his big toe to ensure he is pulling in enough oxygen. In the morning we go home.)

Let the waterfall flow—Victoria Falls and Niagra Falls and all the rest of all the tears that keep needing to be wept. Let them fall. Let them rage. Ban the tacky tourist build-up and the bumper cars. Keep out the vendors and the cure-providing charlatans. Let the rivers flow like holy water raging. Let them sweep away what can't bear the truth. We won't be left with much, but I do take comfort that the God who was with us wept for his friend Lazarus who died. God's tears mingle with ours in this waterfall.

As we wait and hope for the no-more-tears of eternity, may this waterfall become the water the ancient prophet invokes to flow like a justice-and-righteousness-carrying river. While this justice happens in different ways, big and small, I don't have enough faith that it will ever happen on earth nearly as much as it should. But for tears of sadness to be meaningful, certainly they have to join with this river of justice.

I want to cry, because when I'm honest about sadness I'm able to be more open to joy. I want to cry, because maybe it will help me find God. Yes, that might be putting too much added pressure on the tear ducts. I want to cry if it helps me find extra strength for my small work toward justice. If we don't turn away, *just like this* may our tears flow as prayer and then as love.

PART TWO

Searching
for Honest Faith

FAITH IS GRATITUDE. Faith is vulnerable. Faith is humble and does not boast. It is a leap but only toward truth (otherwise it's just a resounding delusion). Faith is hope but not escape. Faith is love for truth, vulnerable to truth, open to truth, being slowly turned toward truth, ready to soar with truth or crash under it. Faith is honest, always honest, and a kind of prayer.

God couldn't be farther—making nonexistence itself a valid possibility. Yet we can also experience God as profoundly, personally present. The truth is at the extremes; the nearness and distance aren't mutually exclusive.

Then there's the claim that two thousand distant years ago God came and walked around in skin and bones. What does this have to do with suffering, with distance, with nearness? Maybe nothing. Maybe everything.

In the Rubble

I ARRIVE FIFTEEN MINUTES into the church service—late in one obvious sense, but I had been there an hour earlier too when nobody had arrived yet, so to my credit, I'd been both early and late. The starting time wasn't firm. The fact they are meeting at all is remarkable.

The church is a pile of rubble. Nothing left. The school beside it is damaged but standing. Nobody had been in the church when it collapsed, but one teacher died in the church school when the roof partially collapsed in his classroom.

The congregation is spread out in three clumps, each trying to find refuge under some kind of shade. One group is under a tree. I join a group of about a hundred people seeking shade near a still-standing outhouse. No room in the shade for this latecomer. I stand listening to the service, singing along to the familiar songs.

I am in the back row with the teenagers. And just to prove that there are some constant universals, even after a staggering natural disaster, even next to a collapsed church building, even with everyone in the congregation now homeless and sleeping outside—the teenagers are whispering, flirting and texting on their phones. It's distracting as I stand sweating, but also funny and comforting. (The world may collapse, but hormones and teenage love endure.)

The service goes on. It is incredible to be singing hymns of praise with them, some of whom I've known for a long time. My faith has always felt buoyed in church here. If our singing voices were made visible as colorful helium balloons released, mine would be straggling at the bottom, holding on to the strings of others for lift. (Even though I of course have the least material excuse for lack of faith of anyone here.) But it does lift—my song, my praise, together.

As the service moves toward Communion, I see Andre, the church deacon I've known since first moving to Haiti, start to make his way across the rubble. After the earthquake, I had walked on the rubble when I first got to town, and it's precarious in spots. I can't figure out what he's doing up there in the middle of the service.

We are moving closer still to Communion, hearing about Jesus with his disciples in the upper room. Andre is up toward the front of the crumbled church now. He is reaching through a tangle of rebar, opening a small concrete cabinet.

Then I realize.

We're singing together about the bread and the wine. "This is Christ's body broken for you. This is Christ's blood shed for you."

Andre pulls out the Communion wafers. The only part of the building or furniture in the church that wasn't smashed to pieces, which I hadn't noticed when I'd been here before, was where they kept the Communion wafers.

Andre is carrying them back over the rubble, each step careful.

"This is my body broken for you."

He makes his way to the rough wood table outside where Communion now happens.

"This is my blood shed for you."

Off to the left is where the teacher died. A ten-minute walk away is where I almost broke down crying as I talked with the mother holding her son, whose father had died saving him.

"This is my body broken for you."

The body of Christ in this place broken, literally broken bodies, broken homes, broken church building.

We line up to go forward and receive. In front of me is a grandmother. She's lost everything and sees her family and community devastated. She's frail. She moves forward without hesitation in the line. A young man behind me. What dreams can he dream now? He keeps moving forward for the bread.

"This is my body broken for you."

I arrive and the jagged Communion wafer—Christ's presence, yes, Christ's presence that did not stop the church from falling, that did not protect the teacher in the school or the dad on the porch, but Christ's presence here in the pile of rubble and here in this group of people in a sun-struck yard—is placed on my tongue.

For the rest of the service I sit on some rocks, still without shade, next to Jean, whose legs are atrophied and folded under him. He can't walk. He's led a tough life with his disability. Before the earthquake, he always sat on the aisle in one of the front rows. When the first chord of the Communion song was struck, the song signaling we could come up front to receive the bread, the song whose chorus is "*Vinn jwenn Jezi, Vinn jwenn Jezi,*" *Come find Jesus, Come find Jesus,* Jean would swing out and, using his hands and arms to propel himself, be first in line. He was always the first to come find Jesus.

And here in the rubble, come find Jesus.

Our God whose distance we don't understand, whose distance we experience as so much suffering and uncertainty and mixed messages. And yet too our God who is right there with Jean first in line and now with people next to a pile of rubble, with their lost loved ones and lost homes down the various paths.

Communion finishes. Andre makes his way back gingerly over the pile to return what is left of the body, broken for us.

The broken God who couldn't feel more distant/near to me in this moment on the rock next to Jean, a jagged Communion wafer dissolving in my stomach.

The rubble seems like evidence of God's absence or abandonment, and yet here I sit, taking and eating the rubbled body of Christ. Here, week after week, people come to find Jesus. The rubble may make him harder to find, but maybe, like the wafers in the center of this leveled church, he never left and never will.

6

KEEP MOVING

How long . . . ?

PSALM 13:2

There's a Sunday school song that I sang growing up and that my daughter has been singing lately:

The foolish man built his house upon the sand . . .
and the house on the sand went splat.

The wise man built his house upon the rock . . .
and the house on the rock stood firm.

It comes from a story told by Jesus, and the *rock,* Jesus explains, is "[hearing] these words of mine and [putting] them into practice" (Matthew 7:24 TNIV). I long understood that the song/story were about choosing the right foundation—and then building a good, solid, concrete house of faith on top of it.

But then life shakes the "house" down to the very foundation. What can you sing when the whole world is unstable ground, when collapse can come in myriad ways from any direction, when mountains can crumble into the sea and neither the rocks nor the sand is always safe? When even faith doesn't seem safe. The metaphor does not inspire my confidence right now; it actually seems to partly undermine Jesus' own point.

Building is too self-protective and static, especially for someone like Jesus who was always on the move and who, the Bible says, had nowhere to lay his head. Instead, Jesus is really talking about himself—living and active—and his words—living and active—and our response—living and active.

A drive through Port-au-Prince goes past the partially collapsed national palace and huge, solid five-story buildings flattened like a stack of pancakes. Then out in the countryside near the epicenter a little wooden peasant house, which looks like it might topple in a stiff wind, still stands among concrete ruins all around. It was often the wood houses—which were flexible—that stayed standing because they shimmied with the shakes.

Some claims to understanding God can seem sturdy on the outside: the engineering is all figured out, the corners tightly measured, the architecture confident and intricate. But any politics, any theologies or ideologies or other -ologies that seem so sure of themselves, that set themselves up as unshakable (Haiti's concrete was bracing for hurricane winds), seem incredibly vulnerable to me as I move through the suffering in Haiti. Instead I try to find comfort in having, like many others, a faith that feels a bit creaky, like the little wooden shack among the towers. Maybe that's not all bad.

My faith in Jesus doesn't always feel secure and unshakable—but it does feel alive. I'm lacking confidence in concrete construction right now, but following after the storyteller, that I can do. Trying to put into practice what I hear? I can do that.

You don't have to have all the answers to climb over the rubble to look for and follow after Jesus. You accept there will be plenty of stumbles and direction changes. Faith/following like this feels like enough—feels honest and alive—to me. And it brings me to life.

◆ ◆ ◆

Gustave is an example of this kind of faith—as he continues to move through awful circumstances with his son, Mike.

The chemo treatment for Mike has already started. There might be a need for a bone marrow transplant. With acute myeloid leukemia, Mike has a fifty-fifty chance of survival.

Two weeks after Mike and Gustave had been evacuated, my wife, Shelly, and I and a couple of other Haitians visited them in Miami Children's Hospital. We had asked what they needed, and Gustave's only requests were a Creole Bible and Haitian food, which we found at a restaurant on the way.

We sat on the floor in the hospital room, speaking Creole and eating rice, beans, *pikliz* and chicken from styrofoam containers. Mike was not eating. He was lying on the bed listlessly, drifting in and out of sleep, with different wires and tubes running in and out of his thin arms. Gustave muted the TV. Larry King was interviewing people about Haiti as B-roll images of the disaster rolled in and out of the commercials.

Gustave joked that when they first arrived at the hospital he couldn't believe they put him on the fourth floor. The first few nights he couldn't sleep for fear of an earthquake. He checked what the ceiling and walls were made of and whether it would be possible to jump out the window if they had to. (No.)

Then he said more seriously, "I don't have a passport and neither does Mike. I don't have a visa or any other papers. I don't have any money. I don't have insurance. I've lost my home. My wife and two daughters are sleeping on the street. My city is destroyed. If we hadn't come here, the doctor said Mike would have died soon. Look around at all this [the tubes and technology]. They give us three meals a day. They take care of Mike. They send someone in to translate for me. How did all this happen? Thank you God."

A Haitian woman who lives in Miami had joined us for the visit, though she didn't know Gustave. An aunt and other friends of hers died in the earthquake. She had been quiet to that point but now spoke up: "You still believe in God?"

"Every morning and every night, I pray with Mike," Gustave answered as he looked at Mike and the room to make his point. His son lying there in dire health, but somehow with world-class care. "I pray and Mike repeats after me. We pray for the rest of our family. And we thank God together."

We had brought a couple of extra meals so Gustave and Mike could have some longed-for Haitian food the next day too. I noticed a little fridge and said we would put them in there.

"Well," Gustave said, "there are some other Haitian families who were evacuated who are just down the hall. They're really missing Haitian food too, so I'll take the rest of this down to them now."

This generosity—it seems to clash with the fact of how much Gustave has lost. The goodness of people who helped Mike get to the United States clashes against the destruction of cancer and the earthquake, without which Mike would have died by now from abnormal cells in his bone marrow and blood. Gustave keeps moving forward with faith.

◆ ◆ ◆

Faith and theology should be flexible, rigorous and alive, like their subject. Otherwise they're a waste.

Simone Weil was a twentieth-century French theologian, philosopher and activist who was always on the move intellectually and engaging, if sometimes clumsily, in the justice issues of her day. She provocatively claimed that we must love truth more than we love Christ.

She loved Christ; this was her way of saying that truth should lead us to love the true Christ. Too often people who love Christ allow him to be shaped so that they end up loving neither the true Christ nor the truth. I want to love both. I want honest faith.

I find Weil's insight helpful for faith in motion, a faith where I don't feel like I'm denying either the truth of God or the truth of everything else we learn and experience. If God is true, then truth ought to repeatedly lead us to God.

So we keep following after Christ and also after truth, so that truth can keep us in check and ensure we're following the right Christ. And we let our faith stay flexible like those wood homes, so that our faith can shimmy with reality and not crumble. When we do this, interacting with Scripture, working to serve other people in need, having new experiences and taking seriously the perspective of others, growing older, connecting with Jesus, facing suffering, seeing the world, and going through crises of faith are all opportunities for our faith to become more honest.

Loving truth means we have to release old beliefs that were wrong or incomplete, which might cause us to grieve. But grieving can be a vital renewing process.

As I watched friends in Haiti, like Emmanuel, the pastor and motorcycle taxi driver, go through what seemed like the well-known stages of grief, my heart ached. One day when we were together he told me with deep self-awareness about his grieving process and how his faith was carrying him through after losing so much.

He articulated the early part of a process that resonated with Elisabeth Kübler-Ross's stages from her 1969 book *On Death and Dying*: denial, anger, bargaining, depression and acceptance. Grief is very personal and not tidy (as both critics and Kübler-Ross herself acknowledge), but it can cycle through some or all of these stages (maybe several times). I wonder if our faith goes through similar cycles as we keep moving and keep loving truth, losing old versions of faith on the way to something new and deeper.

1. *Denial.* When the buildings crashed on 9/11, some people responded in denial: *this can't happen on* our *shores* (though it happens all over the world in different ways). *There's no way we live in a world this brutal.* We might feel pushed to deny reality or deny God. (Cynics might call the early response in Haiti of gratitude to God for the gift of still being alive part of "denial." But then aren't those cynics the ones denying something powerful and tangible in people's faith that clearly carries them forward?)

2. *Anger.* This one's easy. The Psalms brim with anger. I brim with it at times. But I'm not sure churches are great at making space for this. Maybe they're supposed to, maybe not. In some traditions, you have to be so theologically correct that it's hard to be honest about your anger; in others, God is so mysterious or vague that it's hard to get too very angry with metaphors or the ground of one's being.

3. *Bargaining.* Martin Luther (among many others, of course) tried to bargain with God; in his case he wanted God to save him from a violent thunderstorm. You try to see life as a formula that's fair, even though it's not. It's not comfortable to realize how little control you have—of life, of God—so we often try to negotiate along the way.

4. *Depression.* "But I am a worm, and not human" (Psalm 22). It's hard to get out of bed and face a world that is more volatile and indifferent to me than I thought, however I experience God in my life.

5. *Acceptance.* The world isn't what we wish it were. God isn't active in the way we think God should be. But we still experience grace and have reason to believe in God. We're meaner and more selfish and more vulnerable than we want to be. We also experience and have incredible opportunities to give compassion and love. I accept reality and not understanding. I accept and receive the goodness

with gratitude, which seems near the essence of faith.

My faith has cycled through something resembling these stages at different times in my life. Sure it's been uncomfortable at times—and is right now—but I've been exceedingly grateful that this seems like a dynamic relationship with God and truth.

I've also been grateful that I haven't had to go through this alone.

◆ ◆ ◆

If you're still alive, you have to keep on living.

After the earthquake, people had to keep moving forward into each day with some combination of sheer necessity and incredible courage. The structures collapsed, but a mom was still cooking dinner in a pot over a flame in the road median, about five feet wide, as the traffic buzzed by on the only road to the southern peninsula of the country. Others showed up for work—even though they were sleeping on the street—and helped neighbors and made those first efforts to start rebuilding. Of course a few took advantage of the chaos in awful ways, but the vast majority responded with dignity to their own needs and the needs of their neighbors. People also responded generously around the world. You keep moving.

One of the responses that I found surprising and touching was the rush of marriages around the country in the months after the earthquake. Many in Haiti live in common-law marriages because of two significant cultural and economic barriers to a church wedding. First, the man is expected to have a home for his wife, but that is a prohibitive cost, especially when most can't get a mortgage and therefore have to build the home completely with money from earnings. Second, there is an expectation that most will do a church wedding (whether Catholic or Protestant) with a reception that can cost hundreds of dollars or more, when 80 percent of Haitians live on less than two dollars a day.

After the earthquake, suddenly whole swaths of the city and countryside had no homes and there weren't expectations for a reception, so those two barriers, well, collapsed. Then extra motivation came because some Haitians saw the earthquake either as God's judgment on the nation's sinfulness or, even if it wasn't judgment, as an opportunity to get right with God. For these reasons, many couples found post-earthquake to be a good time to make their marriages official and church blessed. In one weekend, three pastors I know were doing multiple-marriage services in their different churches; one married five couples in a single service, another seven couples, and the third eight couples.

Amidst so much sadness, the marriages were, for me, a touching and surprising response. People's heads and hearts were digging out and creating their own stability and commitment in a shaky world.

A bride and groom stand in the sanctuary (or tent) wearing their best available clothes. And in the service there is joy—but not for their honeymoon (there will be none), not for their new home (they'll sleep on the ground under a tarp stamped with an NGO's logo), not for a bounty of gifts (all their friends have lost everything too), not due to the presence of their entire extended family (some are with them, but some were lost under collapsed buildings).

The joy is in feeling right with God. The joy is in receiving the blessing of the church, in giving your friends and community something to celebrate, in reasserting something normal, something that will shimmy with the inevitable shakes, joy in committing to love someone for the rest of your life even when—and even more poignantly because—you know so devastatingly that each day you have together is a kind of unguaranteed grace.

They're finding more strength in their faith when they get to keep moving together.

FROM THE CRUCIBLE

FEODOR DOSTOYEVSKY WROTE THIS in a letter to a friend partway through writing *The Brothers Karamazov:*

> As an answer to all this *negative side* [of the objections raised against God by his character Ivan], I am offering this sixth book, "A Russian Monk." . . . And I tremble for it in this sense: will it be a *sufficient* answer?

Then after the book was published, Dostoyevsky wrote that the entire novel is a response of faith to his own case for atheism. And that the faith that comes out on the other side is all the stronger for it:

> [They] could not even conceive so strong a denial of God as the one to which I gave expression. . . .
>
> Thus it is not like a child that I believe in Christ and confess Him. My hosanna has come forth from the crucible of doubt.

I don't know if God better appreciates the hosannas that have emerged from the crucible, but I trust those hosannas more— whether I hear them being offered up by others or even offered up myself.

7

GOD IS DISTANT AND NEAR

Consider and answer me, O LORD my God!

PSALM 13:3

IT'S A BAD TATTOO AND, as my wife points out, not so bad it's good. Shelly says she'll pay a tattoo artist to improve it if we can find one masterful enough. She says this having spent formative years living on the prison grounds, where her dad was a warden, which instilled the belief that all tattoos are an outward sign of an inward evil.

At least it's on my left shoulder and I don't wear tank tops.

I was in college and wanted a tattoo, so I tried to talk my friend Owen into a tennis wager: If he wins, I buy Gatorade. If I win, we get tattoos. He was a little better than me, so I figured that made the incongruous stakes fair. Except for the part about me buying Gatorade, he thought this was the dumbest idea ever.

I wanted something to mark my faith, despite the Old Testament prohibition. (See Leviticus 19 for rules about tattoos, other obscure laws and a beautiful injunction about loving foreigners "as the citizen.") I lost the tennis match but got a tattoo on my own later that summer. It incorporates three symbols: a heart (for love), an arrow pointing up (for eternity) and a fish (first used by ancient Christians as an identifier and creed in its most basic form; "fish" in Greek is *ichthys,* an acrostic for "Jesus Christ, God's Son, Savior").

I designed it myself, which Owen and Shelly both say is obvious. (The fish symbol wasn't as popular then—not chomping on or being chomped by Darwin on bumper stickers.) Though the aesthetic is bad, I still don't mind that I did it, that it marked my flesh, that it's burned into me. That was probably it: wanting to feel faith and my commitment physically, wanting what is far to come near.

Haitian friends tell me that, in addition to the wave of marriages, their churches are generally overflowing. The same was true in the United States right after 9/11. People are seeking meaning and comfort—maybe the desire to be close to a God who seems far?

There have been revivals all over, some of which have included preaching about end times, sinners in the hands of an angry God, and repentance. I cringe. I'm soft. I want them to keep hearing about the God who is near, for certainly they've experienced God's distance. I want them to hear only words of comfort after all they've been through, and of course that's what many Haitians are saying—save judgment for those complicit, like the Western countries who, from slavery on, too often contributed to their suffering and vulnerability, along with their own exploiting leaders. I want preachers to be preaching God as the Mother Hen taking her chicks under her wings. The prophet Isaiah wrote, "As a mother comforts her child, so I [the LORD] will comfort you." To me the last ones in the world who should stand accused are the 230,001 and all those who remain to pick up the pieces.

I want (though conservative Haitian Protestants wouldn't go for it) to hold up the image of the Pietà—of the mother Mary holding the broken Jesus, beaten and crucified, tenderly holding him across her lap, an image of broken love, love that we can look on with tenderness for the moment and hope because it's on the way to resurrection.

I'm a non-Mary-adoring Protestant, but in a brief stage of writing bad guitar songs in my twenties, I did come up with one lyric that I've held onto as a prayer:

> Jesus, hold me in your Madonna arms;
>> As the damaged man laying across your knees;
>> as the naked newborn who needs to be,
>>> at your breast and in your arms;
> Jesus, hold us in your Madonna arms.

Jesus is at once intimate and aloof in the Gospels. He is God with us, but still there is a distance. The truth isn't in the middle, where I get muddled trying to reconcile things. Instead it seems our experience of God is at these extremes.

To deny the distance (which leaves me skeptically wondering) is to deny how we experience the world. But to deny the nearness (which pulls me further into belief) is to miss out on the truth of Jesus. I don't want to deny either.

◆　◆　◆

We experience God as distant largely because nature is indifferent to us. God's creation interacts with us without concern—providing us with beauty and oxygen and earthquakes and falling trees and pathogens, and sun that makes food grow and sun that causes cancer. It follows the path of sociology and of history, of society's relationship with guns, germs and steel. An earthquake isn't personal; tectonic plates move whether three million people live along that part of the fault line or not. God remains distant, with his presence through the mechanism of this world. If we do happen to experience God's presence in these things—awe at a sunrise or a mountainscape—it's as a connection through distance, not as personal intervention. Nature is wondrous; I think it testifies to God. But through nature we know brutality just as we know beauty. The distance leaves mystery instead of certainty.

One theory is that love requires freedom—and so the distance results from God wanting us to be able to experience and choose love.

Jesus is then the miracle of nearness who, in a physical and mysterious way, drastically closed the distance between God and us, though we still tightrope across by faith.

Through Jesus I do experience God's nearness, even if some days I'm Peter, denying Jesus in different (though less interesting or less high-stake) ways. Other days I'm Pilate, dismissing Jesus with a kind of cowardly neglect. I wear a flimsy little crown on my own proud head at times, and isn't that a bit like putting a crown of thorns on his? Other times I am (even in this book) like the "bad thief" on the cross, knowing my own guilt and yet lashing out in hopes of provoking a reaction, any reaction, from the God who is hanging there while we all die. Occasionally I'm one of the women at the foot of the cross, briefly courageous, heartbroken for the pain of it all. Maybe I aspire to be simply the good thief, contrite, not expecting much, embarrassed by my guilt but hoping for his grace. But instead of just "Remember me," it's a prayer of "Remember us" as the aftershocks continue.

I stay a Christian because I find that Jesus brings God near—to me, to us. I affirm with as full conviction as I know that Jesus is the incarnate One, both God and human, who lived and died and rose from the dead, who is Savior and Lord, who will judge by grace, and who will somehow bring into being a new life just as real as all the suffering. It's a simple, wavering faith but not in something floofy and metaphorical. If I'm going to believe, especially when real people are really crushed, then for me the only worthwhile faith is in something exceedingly real.

Each Easter I like to read John Updike's beautiful poem "Seven Stanzas at Easter." It begins:

> Make no mistake: if he rose at all
> It was as His body;
> If the cell's dissolution did not reverse, the molecule reknit,
> The amino acids rekindle,
> The Church will fall.

Through the poem Updike, this writer of the American suburbs, is concerned most with scientific modernity's assault on faith in the resurrection. I can identify with these doubts, but he asserts they shouldn't embarrass us into unbelief. The stanzas of the poem articulate the kind of faith I need in response to Haiti, where so many died (by comparison, a similar-intensity earthquake in Los Angeles in 1994 killed only seventy-two people) largely because they had been left behind in poverty by the modern world.

I nod Amen with him, as the physical specificity of faith (of the Savior) must respond to the physical, concrete rubble that I drive past in Haiti, as well as the physically decomposed bodies I see even months later being uncovered and put into plastic bags that are thrown into the back of dump trucks:

> Let us not mock God with metaphor,
> Analogy, sidestepping, transcendence,
> Making of the event a parable, a sign painted in the faded
> Credulity of earlier ages:
> Let us walk through the door.
>
> The stone is rolled back, not papier-mâché,

Not a stone in a story,
But the vast rock of materiality that in the slow grinding of
Time will eclipse for each of us
The wide light of day.

Walking "through the door" makes sense as a description of faith, more so to me than the famous definition in Hebrews 11: "being sure of what we hope for and certain of what we do not see" (TNIV). That definition isn't particularly helpful for me (which is my deficit, I'm sure, and not that of Scripture). Because of God's distance/nearness, I wish the writer of Hebrews had gone more in the *Merriam-Webster's* uncertain-but-still-committed definition: "firm belief in something for which there is no proof."

We can also try for a definition of faith via antonyms: Faith is the opposite of doubt, despair, fear, credulity, atheism, certainty, skepticism? All these make some sense to me as opposites, and I experience each of them battling with my faith at times, so it seems unnecessary to claim just one.

But I'm also fighting for the anger, doubt and sadness to be part of—instead of opposed to—faith. I see that, and want to be more like what I see, in the Psalms and in Blaise by that roadside cooler and in those kids laughing and shaking their fists in the aftershocks. Faith "walks through the door" and engages with God and other people.

Faith like this is a kind of following, and following is, of course, trying to get closer to something or someone (or at least trying not to fall any farther behind). I can follow Jesus even if he sometimes seems elusive or disappears over a mound of rubble. Faith that doesn't keep seeking dies, and the distance between God and us seems to expand. If I still have a measure of hope and gratitude, I can follow, though I'm full of fear or doubt, though I'm angry or disappointed.

God took on a body to be close with us and so we could be closer to God. We need this because God is also mysterious and because God's creation is impervious—that is, without any care one way or the other (like in the case of little Mike, and what nature is carelessly doing to his body).

It's up to each person whether to get tattoos to feel the physicality of all this along the way, but if you do, I'd recommend consulting with a professional.

◆　◆　◆

A few months after that first visit when I'd worshiped outside with the church, I am able to return to Darbonne on a Sunday.

This time we sit under a tarp for worship. It's warm but not too sweaty yet. The tarp is over the foundation where the rubble has been cleared, the concrete cabinet holding the Communion wafers still stands.

The need of so many families is still stunning. The shell of the school building still teeters on the left, even more precariously now. Jagged gray piles, leftover buildings, are to the right. A ramshackle rusted tin home is just up ahead. Many people on the benches now have tarps or tents, but continue to be without homes or much else. Yet they continue to gather together, dressed in their best clothes, singing to God with passion.

It's Pentecost Sunday—when we celebrate that God's Holy Spirit came down after the resurrected Jesus ascended to heaven. The claim is that God's nearness continues even after Jesus left. I believe more when I'm here. Presumably because I'm surrounded by faith and courage amid circumstances that seem most likely to leave faith and courage in a crumbled heap.

Jean still swings out first and drags himself up for Communion. We all follow. Christ's body, still broken for us. Christ's body, a distant God come near to us. After Communion is done, Jean gets down, pulls himself over to me and asks if I have any money.

"Let's wait till after the service," I whisper.

God seems nearer because I'm here with people who believe in the Holy Spirit today. God seems nearer when I can take the bread and wine. God seems nearer because Jean is first in line—and then he comes over and reminds me what love is (if you want to love God, you have to love me, he might as well say).

As we sit under the tarp, no walls, just open to the surrounding area, I don't even have to swivel my head to look directly at some of the most compelling testimony in the past hundred years for God's distance. Yet here I sit with people who are believing and experiencing, through faith, God's nearness.

And so am I.

MEMENTO MORI

Just before the earthquake, Père, the grandfather of the Woshdlo family I first lived with in Haiti, pulled me aside to tell me about the latest project he was starting. As usual he was barefoot, in tattered slacks and a partly shredded button-down shirt that he wears for work in his fields.

He said he had been saving up to make a burial place—a small, traditional concrete tomb. The time was coming closer, he said, and he wanted to prepare for his death so the costs didn't fall to his children.

When I was there after the earthquake, I saw the big, square hole in the ground (maybe ten feet by ten feet, and about six feet deep) about twenty paces from his home.

It reminded me of two snippets I heard and extrapolated about different monasteries:

At a secluded, countryside monastery every monk—as a ritual each morning—goes in the early dawn hours to the brothers' cemetery. On arrival, each one grabs from the shed the rough wooden handle of a shovel. Then walks over to sink that shovel a single time into his own predesignated grave.

The first days it's as though they're not making a difference at all. A newly installed brother might get only a loose, light shovelful of grass and topsoil. The wind blows dirt and leaves to cover the first digs of mortality. But some weeks in, the faint form of a grave takes shape, a hole shaped for a body, for the digger's body. But still only inches deep.

Eventually, decades into their life and work, senior monks (sometimes with the help of a younger brother) climb gingerly down a ladder into the grave and dump a shovelful of the dark, moist, heavy dirt into a bucket, which is then hoisted up the ladder before the monk slowly, rung by rung, emerges from the hole that he will one day descend into without coming back up.

One shovelful at a time, closer to death. One more shovelful alive.

More vocal and less physical (and less practical), at another monastery monks greet each other, whenever they pass and it is not an hour of silence, with the phrase, *"Memento mori." Remember you will die.*

This instead of, "Hi. How are you?"

It serves the same purpose as the shovel. I'd find it less helpful as a ritual to reflect on life and death. But it might be a more effective spiritual discipline for living: Can you imagine how hard it would be on some days to not say *"Memento mori"* with secret satisfaction to a particularly annoying colleague?

Each Ash Wednesday, if you go to a church that does this sort of thing, a version of *memento mori* happens when you go to your knees and a cross of ashes is marked on your forehead as you hear the words, "Remember that you are dust and to dust you will return."

The curse is on skin and bones, but so too comes the blessing.

8

JESUS

(CRUCIFIX VERSUS CROSS)

Give light to my eyes, or I will sleep the sleep of death, . . .

my foes will rejoice because I am shaken.

PSALM 13:3-4

A SYMBOLICALLY POTENT PHOTO circulated via email soon after the earthquake. Maybe because I've been manipulated by too many movies and Photoshopped ads, it didn't initially move me as it might have.

In the picture, a six-foot-tall crucifix made of concrete (not wood) stands unfallen in front of the crumbled concrete of Sacre Coeur (Sacred Heart) Catholic Church in downtown Port-au-Prince. The black iron fence in front of it is bent and broken. Collapsed concrete blocks are piled around it. In the background is a church ruined, with only parts of disintegrated walls and crumpled tin roofing still holding together.

Jesus hangs there on the smooth concrete cross, untouched by the earthquake but with nails in his hands and feet, a crown of thorns stuck in his scalp.

Jesus—the only thing that stays standing when the
    world crumbles
Jesus—untouched by the suffering as the world falls
    around him
Jesus—suffering with us
Jesus—worship all you want, it makes no difference in real life
Jesus—a Savior in the middle of real life, in the rubble
    and suffering

The difference between a Protestant cross and a Catholic crucifix is the absence/presence of Jesus' tortured, limp body. The explanation I vaguely remember is that they reflect the different emphases between justification from sins through the resurrection (Protestants; no body) and God's presence through suffering and sacrifice (Catholics; body), though I'm sure this is too simplistic.

I'm very Protestant. I've visited Catholic churches in the United States and attended them regularly in Haiti, but whenever I start thinking I'm kind of Catholic I realize it's in a thoroughly pick-and-choose Protestant way.

That said, the crucifix works better for me as a way to enter prayer, worship and gratitude. The doubt and the suffering are right there with the implied hope. I'm all for the hope of resurrection—but the Protestant cross is too sanitized. Though the suffering of the empty cross is acknowledged, it's left behind with the risen body. But we haven't, ourselves, left that suffering behind. We're in it.

I saw the photo again recently. It made me want to face the cross. So I went looking in my town in Florida and found two, one at a Catholic church and one at a Protestant one.

◆ ◆ ◆

Jesus, on the cross:

Jesus,

My questions still hang there with your body. Each time they arise in my spirit, I don't know whether they're going to rise again with you or not. Your head hanging to the right. Your rib cage protruding. A final breath exhaled.

Why, Jesus? To be so close with us, to know the agony and the joy. To eat the fish, to attend weddings, to raise the dead. To feel tears down your cheek. But then you left, even if you did leave alive.

I'm in such awe looking here at your body, but I feel such disappointment. Not in you. You gave everything. In your life you showed love and healing, you revealed hypocrisy and revealed truth. In your death you showed forgiveness of all kinds, a profound kind of hope for people, with much need for forgiveness—because of what we've done, because of what has been done to us.

You hang here in your moment of death.

One other person is here now, eight pews up. In her blue blouse, she's up and down from her knees. Her shoulders turned down and in toward her chest as though trying to shield her heart.

It's hot in here and dark. No air conditioning, no fans, little light. The air is stale. In the quiet. You. Bathed in the light. You make complete sense there, but you look out of place the way they've glorified you on this cross with gold embellishments—glorified at your most painfully human. Though maybe that's the point.

Forgive me, Jesus. The gold on your cross is gaudy. I'm petty. And then when I'm serious, I hurl accusations at you, though I toss rocks as a guilty one who doesn't do enough to help other people who are suffering.

I feel achingly alone in this silence. I might be alone. But if, God, you were there in that body, then you are the God for me. Broken.

Not a clockmaker tinkering and then watching it unfold at a safe distance. I mean, you seem like that too, but then here you are, a body pierced and bruised and bloodied.

I don't know why you needed to do this. Were your hands pierced so you could be the God of the little boy I met recently whose arm was newly amputated (maybe without any anesthesia), a stub just below his elbow?

That would be reason enough.

Did you come so you could love better, in the way we do when we taste the suffering or perspective of others? I can't remember the heresies that question would get filed under, but short of rescuing us, that is another way to love that I can understand.

Did you come to save us from the other part of yourself, the holy Judge whose punishment for us would be severe? We can be so evil but we're also a bunch of feeble things. Yes, I want judgment Old-Testament-style meted out on the unjust, on those (except myself) who exploit or neglect the helpless or anyone for that matter. If all this was to save us from your own holiness, I understand the theory but it doesn't completely make sense to me—but I'm grateful for any saving we can get.

The temple curtain was ripped top to bottom in this moment, your final breath. Distance dramatically comes near. But somehow it seems to have been sewn back together over the years.

Keep ripping the curtain down that we might know you. In this final breath it does seem you know us. And so even love us.

Amen.

◆　◆　◆

Jesus, gone from the cross:

Jesus,
You're not here. Not on the cross. Hard to find elsewhere sometimes too. Your cross here in front of me is made of marble, not even

wood. The pews are empty. After praying to you in front of a crucifix this seems harder—the story here is the hope but, searching through suffering and doubt, it's hard not to first be struck simply by your absence.

The pews are wood with blue padding. The sun is diffused through the windows. The marble cross is smooth, milky white. Unadorned in any other way.

You've gone to prepare mansions for us in your Father's kingdom, you say. I know a lot of people right now who would be willing to accept something much simpler than a mansion if it would protect them from the muck and disease of rain.

But here's the thing I don't get: so many people in the rain who trust you. I know their faith in you is greater than mine and their expectations of you seem lower. Not that they think less of you or that you're able to do less but . . . I don't know.

Some are crushed. A friend outside Port-au-Prince is sleeping with her two children under a tarp. Her first husband beat her, her second husband died. She's young still. When I just visited she told me her third child, a two-and-a-half-year-old son, died the month before of "a fever."

When you're on the cross, you suffer with us. I need that. But if your body was taken down and then you rose, if your Spirit is both around us here, now, and out there somehow in eternity, then I do find hope in that of course.

Your body hanging limp on the cross: it means something that you suffered with us, but if I'm stuck in a deep pit then I don't really care if someone who walks by is in solidarity with me or not. I just want them to help me out.

These two crosses, in faith, are hoping for both: that you'll be down in it with us, that you'll pull us out.

Your poet David said, "[God] lifted me out of the slimy pit, out of the mud and mire, . . . set my feet on a rock and gave me a firm place to stand." You prepared a way for us, but the way too often still feels like slimy clay. Or insecure concrete. Or flimsy wood.

I find hope. It's what I find exasperating about you. That the promise is so much, that the hope is so incredible, that you knew our weakness, that you offered your side to be touched by Thomas and knew it would be harder for us now. Your body now gone. A matter of faith now.

And another thing that drives me crazy: When I only want to doubt or dismiss you, I can't help being drawn to you and finding strength and hope in you. Like Enel with everyone in the square that earthquake night.

Yet when I want to surrender to you in faith, so much around cries out that the story is insane, that the hope is too great to be true, that so much is ambiguous.

My hope on good days resembles faith in you, the one whose body no longer hangs here. If you're just an idea, metaphor, analogy, parable, remnant of ancient credulity, I'm not interested. If your resurrection is anything but materially true, then the idea is admirable but I'm needing something more real and straightforward—otherwise it seems useless to pray to God in your name.

I'm left not knowing what to pray. But because your body once hung on a cross like this (well, not three feet tall and marble on a wall, but you know what I mean) and because your body is no longer hanging on a cross I ask:

May doubt win where it is true.
Likewise may faith win where there is something real to
    trust.

And may that faith be:

That God's love is stronger than suffering.

That God's love is stronger than death.

That the unredeemable suffering all around will somehow be redeemed.

Amen.

◆　◆　◆

God comes embodied to humanity in a number of religions. Jesus is the way Christians believe God came to us. Paul understood it this way:

> Let the same mind be in you that was in Christ Jesus,
>> who, though he was in the form of God,
>>> did not regard equality with God
>>> as something to be exploited,
>> but emptied himself,
>>> taking the form of a slave,
>>> being born in human likeness.
> And being found in human form,
>> he humbled himself
>> and became obedient to the point of death—
>> even death on a cross. (Philippians 2:5-8)

The distant God comes intimately, vulnerably close and—from up on the cross—invites us to follow in a way that is humble and serving and vulnerable. Not as suicide, but to help others facing their own kind of crucifixions.

I had long thought the cross was just about being loved by God, but as I prayed before the two versions, saw it standing surrounded by rubble, laid my anger and doubts before it, put my faith up on it, knew something about God's love for us, listened to Paul, I heard again that, yes, it *is* about God loving us—but quicker than I wish, it becomes not just about how I can find God, but how I'm supposed to give love, and how we have to find God together.

THE MUD

THE RAIN ROARS DOWN. That season has arrived. The rain might as well be tears, drenching hundreds of thousands of people in tents and under tarps.

I'm back staying with the Woshdlo family as I check on the rebuilding progress in our nearby schools. The family is all in one home talking and telling stories while waiting out heavy rain. The provisional house is holding. Père, the grandfather, comes and goes in these times. He won't sit for too long. Having lived on this plot of land for sixty-seven years, he is long past letting rain paralyze him, even if he understands that the rest of his extended family prefers to stay dry.

Eventually he comes to get me. It's late and everyone is ready to sleep. Though I could find my own way, Père wants to escort me to the little room in the provisional tin house where I'll sleep.

We slog together through mud and water at least a foot deep. It's slippery, so I lose and then retrieve a flip-flop a few times. Occasional lightning makes the path clear. We arrive at the little porch of the house and I'm getting ready to go in when Père stoops down to where he had put a bucket of water. Suddenly my foot is cradled in his hand and he's gently washing off the mud.

I protest. No, I'll do it. No, please don't, Père. But there's something holy about it. Of course I think of Jesus washing the disciples' feet and their protesting. I'm humbled to silence. Père isn't doing this because he's subservient or feels like he has to. For more than seven years I've watched his humility, generosity and kindness.

The fruits of the Spirit listed in Galatians 5:22 have seemed too soft and too reinforcing of the status quo to me since realizing what the world is like. "Love, joy, peace, patience, kindness, generosity, faithfulness, gentleness, and self-control" is a great list, but not enough. It should also include, based on other parts of the Bible, "risky compassion, discomfort with the comfortable, defiance in the face of injustice." Read in a middle-class church, the original list can just strengthen self-satisfaction and complacency. Sure, it's not easy to be all those things in your marriage or with colleagues or neighbors, but it's a lot easier than giving up what I have to engage with people who are poor or challenging the very systems that help make life good for my family. The fruit of the Spirit—the fruit of being shaped to be more like Jesus—has to be more revolutionary.

I think about how I'm supposed to follow Jesus to love more—but then of course here I am, humbled and being loved far more than I can love. In thirty years, when I'm Père's age, I hope I've become a little of the man he is. I look up to him in every way. I balance now on my clean foot just inside the doorway as he washes the mud covering my other foot.

He is full of dignity, confidence, stubbornness. He gets angry and yells at himself or just in general or occasionally at the grandkids when they're disobedient—but always still with a twinkle in his eye.

I don't want my soul shaped by the market or the latest technology or pride. I don't want my ambition or my fears to shape me. I want to make a difference and support the right causes, but they're not enough either.

Let the philosophers and scientists and skeptics mock; even though I'd like to be more sophisticated—and it is more complex than this—I'll just say what's true as I'm here in the rain with Père: I believe in Jesus in part because Père believes. And I even believe in that revolutionary kingdom that Jesus says has come and is coming in and around us.

The same was true many a morning at 5 a.m., when only the

9

THE RESPONSE IS US

But I trusted in your steadfast love.

PSALM 13:5

I<small>T WAS LIKE THE WORLD WAS ENDING</small> . . . but then Jesus didn't show up."

A friend told me this several years ago after his family and members from his church had huddled in his small hilltop house outside the city of Jacmel, Haiti, during a hurricane. His was the sturdiest of the village's homes. His younger daughter cried through the night's frightening roar of wind and rain. His older daughter sang hymns along with everyone else. In the morning when they could venture out, their homes, gardens and livestock were wrecked. Their world ended in a way, but they were left to recover, not taken up in glory.

After the earthquake, three other friends told me the same thing in slightly different ways. They're people of profound faith. How could you not think the world was ending if you were downtown in Port-au-Prince that day?

"It was like the world was ending . . . but then Jesus didn't show up."

◆ ◆ ◆

When extreme suffering happens, God doesn't swoop in for the super-hero rescue or with kingdom come or as manna raining down from heaven for the hungry. Instead Jesus says that God shows up through us. While that's flattering, it often seems like yet another deep flaw in the system—like our faith in God fails at the same time that we fail at the expectations God has of us. The failures reinforce each other.

But when our lives crash, this is also often true: "It was like the world was ending and Jesus didn't show up . . . but then God did, when _____ came and was so kind." A stranger. A friend. Offering encouragement or a meal, a job or a room to stay in.

God performs jujitsu in response to our questions about suffer-ing—our protests are not answered but are instead redirected back at us *and we are made responsible.* As Jesus got ready to leave for good after the resurrection, he said, "Very truly, I tell you, the one who believes in me will also do the works that I do and, in fact, will do greater works than these, because I am going to the Father." So the follower will do works that are as good as—and even better—than Jesus. Be-cause Jesus is multiplied now through thousands and millions of us. We're supposed to love like little Christs. Belief should trigger our helping others in a way related to how Jesus loved people.

The suffering question is theological and the answer is ethical. This is the divine jujitsu. "Why suffering?" comes back at us as "Help each other in your suffering." People are supposed to experience God's love through others showing up to help. And Jesus says some-thing else happens too: those who help actually experience Jesus in the one they're helping.

When Enel stumbled out of the collapsed university and was helped down to the square where he rested, when the man came with water to wipe his face caked in dust and to give him a drink that helped him make it through that first night, Jesus was there in two ways:

Enel experienced Jesus as the man who gave him water to drink. The man who gave Enel water experienced Jesus in Enel (a real-life dramatization of the story Jesus tells in Matthew 25).

In other words, where there is love in a moment of need, Jesus is there in the shared space between them. Because love is there.

This God who is distant comes close through . . . us. *Practically* when we're clearing rubble, when we're healing wounds, when we're helping people create their own better future, when we're working to overturn unjust systems and provide where there is need. *Mystically* because in this practical help we experience something of the transcendent God's presence.

◆ ◆ ◆

Mike spent two months at Miami Children's Hospital and was then transferred to Phoenix Children's Hospital. Gustave told me he was nervous about this. He was moving farther from, instead of closer to, his wife and two young daughters, who were still in Haiti sleeping outside with other neighbors and extended family.

But once Mike and Gustave were in Phoenix, a team formed around them to take care of them and work toward reuniting their family (partly because Mike's two sisters were potential bone marrow donors). It started with his sponsoring charity and a dedicated oncologist, and then grew to include people with connections in the Haitian and American governments and an entrepreneur with a private plane ready to pick up the rest of the family in Haiti. I've never heard of a visa process moving so fast. Shelly and I played a small role by becoming the sponsors of Gustave's wife and two daughters; our paperwork, tax returns and signed promises to the U.S. government helped keep the process moving.

Mike, vulnerable from the leukemia and chemo, got a fungal infection in his lungs soon before his mother and sisters were cleared to receive visas and travel to the United States. He was in critical condition, sedated, with a tube down his throat. How much could his weakened four-year-old body take? From conversations with Gustave and email updates from others in the week before his family arrived, I wondered if the doctors were at the point of just trying to keep Mike alive until his mom could arrive to say goodbye to him. Gustave told me that, though he felt bad doing so, he wasn't telling his wife the whole truth about Mike's condition; he didn't think she could handle it at a distance.

Some, not all, of the team around Mike believe in God. Some, not all, are Christians. None of them knew Mike or Gustave before the earthquake. They are a remarkable example of committed love in their help for this little boy.

When there is a disaster of shocking scale like in Haiti, people often long to find a tangible way to enter into it. It's much easier, as Sara the ER nurse said, to "enter the room" if you can make a difference. People's responses seem to come both from compassion (a desire to help) and from their existential wrestling (as a way to try to fight off or make meaning of suffering itself). Both these reasons are part of why I've chosen my work. When we have faith, we should ask the *why* questions of suffering, but the search for answers has to be while working on the *how* responses against it.

Maybe, with little Mike, we can defeat suffering *in this one boy.* At least we're in a potentially winnable fight for good, even if we know it doesn't always win.

◆ ◆ ◆

Jesus said, "Believe me that I am in the Father and the Father is in me; but if you do not, then believe me because of the works themselves." Then later, "By this everyone will know that you are my disciples, if you have love for one another."

On the surface Jesus' claim is rebutted easily on musty campus couches and wherever else Christianity is debated with responses like, "But Gandhi was more about love and peace and more Jesus-like than most Christians." Some of the main people who helped Mike weren't doing it in any way for Jesus. Works of love aren't actually proof. They require interpretation of faith too. Christians can love and serve incredibly. But studies have shown that many in the United States would complete the sentence, "They will know we are Christians by our _____" with the word *judging*.

In these debates Christians can play offense and point out all the good things Christians have done through history, which would be fair. Or they can get defensive and say that the numerous wars, genocides, child rapes and so on were not by real Christians and were sin hidden under a banner of false justification, which is kind of true but kind of squirrely.

None of those arguments touch me, though. They're *out there;* they're a mix of good and evil, beauty and horror. I know people transformed by faith in ways that are good and deep and true, but I also know plenty of Christians marked just as much by sin and selfishness (and I count myself among them). History isn't relative, yet its complexity seems to yield only a Rorschach test that reveals the faith of the beholder and not proof of God.

But I do know this: I find more meaning and comfort, and I'm better at giving goodness and love, because of Jesus' effect on me. It's an important reason for why I work in Haiti. It's part of why I keep finding myself converted again and again from indifference or disbelief to belief, for a day, for this moment.

Before a recent visit to Haiti, I received a text message from someone in our Woshdlo family. Her text in Creole said, *Each time I hear you're coming it's like Christ coming to work in our home and for our family.*

It made me shudder. I tried to forget it quickly. I know that I'm not generous enough, that I could do more, that I must disappoint them regularly. We're close and we give a lot to each other, but they deserve more than me.

Is this humility—or me trying to avoid the full responsibility?

We're not supposed to be the saviors (for extreme examples, see how horribly wrong colonialism and neocolonialism went). But we each can be humble, flawed gap-fillers between God's absence and presence. The Woshdlo family, with Père and the others, is Christ to me in many ways when I visit them, but I'd like to avoid having to be Christ to them.

While living in Haiti it was disconcerting to find love being re-defined for me. Growing up, love consisted of things like giving time, being truthful, not betraying confidence, helping out, show-ing generous interest, demonstrating faithfulness, being patient and kind and forgiving. First Corinthians 13 kind of love (the "love is patient, love is kind" that gets read at weddings).

In Haiti, though, Shelly and I were in relationships where love, if it was love, was significantly less emotional/poetic and more crassly transactional. Money was often the currency. Sometimes people wanted my money, but it had nothing to do with me as a person (who wants to be loved in return). "Love is being an ATM" isn't the stuff of Shakespeare or slow-burn R&B records or Sandra Bullock movies.

We found that the neighbor needs money for his niece's funeral far more than a shoulder to cry on. And while it may have been empha-sized because we were foreigners, something similar (but obviously more complex and fuller) happened between Haitians I knew in the countryside who were poor. Soon into discussions of romance came the question of whether the man gave the woman good, regular money, because that was an indication of the seriousness of the love.

Over time I better understood how the emphasis of love should be meeting each other's needs in different ways, whether the love is romantic or between friends or neighbors. This way of loving as an exchange can be dehumanizing for everyone involved, but it can also be more real and lasting than purely poetic love.

I'm not Christlike—but I am more like Jesus because Jesus is part of my life. Despite my selfishness, I'm a little less so because I think Jesus' presence has changed something in my life. I still get depressed and struggle to find meaning sometimes, but less so because I find hope in Jesus. I can certainly still be a coward, but I take some risks on behalf of others that I wouldn't take if I weren't inspired by Jesus to do so. I could write pages about just my failures in loving well, but I think I love better because of knowing something about God's love in Jesus.

It's not that I couldn't be a good person without Jesus; obviously many people are good (much better than I am) who don't believe in God at all or who follow other religions. Actually, a high percentage of the best international aid workers I've known—who give themselves with dedication and insight, who make a real difference for people suffering acutely—are agnostics. But for me, the connection with God in faith makes an immeasurable difference in my life.

I think what I believe is true; otherwise I would abandon my faith. What I've experienced doesn't prove God's existence to anyone else (it barely does for me some days), but it does keep holding onto me and moving me forward.

A friend of the writer Henri Nouwen tells the story of someone angry with him, after he was rude once, who confronted him questioning the disconnect between his actions and his faith. Nouwen was heartbroken and said, "I wonder if [he] ever considered what I would be like if I wasn't a man of prayer."

The Holy Spirit, which is the most mysterious part of the Trinity, is also the most prosaic as it absorbs our protests about suffering and then responds (at least I believe it does) by whispering, jujitsu-like, into the echoes of our doubt an unsatisfying but demanding and ultimately hopeful answer:

I love you.

I love you.

I love you.

I love you.

I love you.

I love you.

I love you.

I love you. (I suffer with you when you suffer.)

I love you.

I love you.

I love you.

I love you.

I love you.

I love you. (I breathe your every breath.)

I love you.

I love you.

I love you.

I love you.

I love you.

I love you.

I love you.

I love you. (Your life means as much as you hope it does.)

I love you.

I love you.

I love you.

I love you.

I love you.

I love you.
I love you. (And so I am distant.)
I love you.
I love you.
I love you.
I love you.
I love you.
I love you.
I love you. (And so I am near.)
I love you.
I love you.
I love you.

Now go and love.

ACTION OF GRACE

AFTER ENEL HAD DUG HIMSELF out of the rubble of his collapsed university and then collapsed himself in the public square, after the night of singing and praying in the midst of a ruined city, Enel lay there the next morning as one traumatized among many. A friend happened to walk by and recognize him. He helped Enel to a clinic and then eventually home to the island of La Gonâve.

Haiti is shaped like a horseshoe, with two long peninsulas forming a bay in the middle. Enel lives on the large island in the middle of this bay. Getting to his home requires riding a boat to the island—which has about one hundred thousand residents, many of whom struggle to extract life from the landscape—and then long, punishing dirt roads. It's a tiring trip in the best of health.

The doctor said Enel had no serious internal injury. His family nursed him back to health. In a week he started walking with a makeshift cane. Then, as soon as he was able (and to the protest of his friends and family), he was back regularly in Port-au-Prince, sleeping in a tent on the streets, to start doing his small part of the work for his country's recovery.

A month after the earthquake, Enel held an *Aksyon de Gras* (Action of Grace) service back on the island. I hadn't heard of this before, and he hadn't ever been to one, but church friends had told him about them. The services are part of church culture, he said, and something similar is sometimes held in voodoo.

Enel invited the local community and nearby churches to the service. He had bought five hundred paper plates to use in feeding everyone; seven hundred people came. It cost a lot, but he had life itself to celebrate and be grateful for. This was his gratitude to God. For three hours everyone worshiped, prayed, sang, and ate rice, yams, a traditional mix of vegetables and meat, and drank juice made from local oranges.

During the service was the first time that Enel wept after the earthquake. (Crying as "signaling" is definitely part of this service.) He was personally grateful but made sure that that overflowed into the community. It was a celebration of life—but of course any celebration of life in the weeks after the earthquake was also a grieving for the dead.

"I think it was contentment that made me cry," he told me. "Of course there is all kinds of sadness still too. I don't know exactly what I was feeling at that moment. I was feeling so much. This is all beyond me. My family and children were there. My community. I was rejoicing to God. I was overwhelmed with crying."

The service celebrated a kind of resurrection, while acknowledging that so many were left out. Enel feels a weight of responsibility with the reprieve he's been given.

It's complex being grateful for grace in this world. How to be grateful to God for what you receive when the person next to you goes without? I sometimes spin around and around like I'm on a roulette wheel, moving between gratefulness, disappointment toward God and survivor's guilt.

But as much as it's possible to decide, it seems best to pause most often on gratitude. Gratitude can be genuine though conflicted, just as faith can be committed though uncertain. (And gratitude seems close to the essence of faith.)

Enel didn't understand what had happened or why. He, his wife, and their young daughter and son knew only to receive it as a gift and a responsibility.

10

HONEST FAITH

My heart shall rejoice in your salvation.

I will sing to the LORD,

because he has dealt bountifully with me.

PSALM 13:5-6

M<small>IKE HAD JUST BEEN RELEASED</small> from the hospital two days before I arrived to visit him and his family in Phoenix, Arizona, six months after the initial medical evacuation to Miami. There are pockets of progress in Haiti and we work with inspiring partners, but the overall situation is still dire, with more than a million people still homeless.

Yet when I walk into their apartment, little Mike is sitting on the floor watching cartoons, ready with a big smile and a high five. (Gustave and I have discovered we both have children who like SpongeBob, which is yet another mystery of the highest order.) Michelette, Djenika and Carla are there too. They finally arrived two weeks ago.

Mike has finished his fourth and final round of chemo. Squiggly hairs are reappearing on his bald head. He's fragilely thin and walks with a limp from weakness after spending much of the previous month in bed with the lung infection. Before medical advances in the past ten years, this infection would have killed him.

Destroying the leukemia meant killing his already compromised immune system. A nurse in blue scrubs comes to the apartment to ensure that Gustave is properly administering the medicine into Mike's right arm through the "PICC line" (a peripherally inserted central catheter that runs a small IV-like tube up through the vein in his arm to a main vein near his heart, where the blood flows quickly, thereby applying medicine most effectively). The nurse tells me, "Mike is vulnerable to disease like one of us would be to danger when standing alone outside on the top of a skyscraper as a category five hurricane roars through."

Later at the hospital, I talk with Mike's oncologist who says that at the time he was evacuated from Port-au-Prince, Mike was extremely close to death (probably from some kind of infection) because the disease had progressed to the point that his bone marrow was only producing leukemia-affected cells. His bloodstream had been populating with cells that would kill rather than protect him.

With the leukemia now out of his system, the focus for the next year becomes hoping the leukemia doesn't return and helping to protect Mike and rebuild his immune system. To make him less vulnerable.

◆　◆　◆

On the plane to visit Mike and his family, the man next to me, about twenty-five years old, and I didn't talk till we were taxiing to the gate. Sleeping and reading took priority.

"You coming on business or vacation, or coming home?" I asked.

"Just back from Iraq, actually," he said.

"Oh, you're in the military? How was it? What were you doing?"

"No. At a funeral."

"A friend in the military die?"

"No, my older brother's wife and children died in a car accident there. It's where my family is from. I was there with him for the funeral."

The reminders of our vulnerability are relentless: a tragedy, a ravaged immune system, an earthquake, a child drowning in a pool (last week's headline), a family torn apart. I feed my children birdlike bites because about seventy children in the United States die each year from choking on food; it's a tiny percentage but still frightening. Meanwhile about seventeen thousand children in the world die *each day* from lack of nutrition.

Cells and suffering metastasize around us with abandon. And it's like in the end we're just left . . . to protest, to trust?

I've been writing this book because my faith might die. I don't want it to. But I don't want a sentimental faith. I didn't know where this search would lead, whether I would be able to claw my way to gratitude as at the end of Psalm 13. I *do want* any part of my faith that isn't true to die. I don't want to close my eyes to anything about this world. I hate a lot about this world. I'm writing this so I can find a way to love God with more of my heart—this heart that God created to know much joy and love, but that will also be crushed again and again.

At the same time I'm grateful beyond measure for the goodness of life, which I can't prove but still receive as a gift from God. So maybe I have found my way to gratitude, but it doesn't feel as unrestrained as those last verses of the psalms often do.

I want to see through the window clearly, but it's stained and streaked blurry. I want to know without having to jump off the balcony. I want to know before eternity arrives or doesn't. I want love now. I don't want to turn away. I want to cry if it leads to love and joy—or even just truth. I don't just have survivor's guilt; I am guilty of not doing enough to help some who might have survived. I need courage to give more. I know that I need forgiveness as much as I long for justice.

◆ ◆ ◆

For anyone who wants to be hoped for in these ways:

I hope that, individually and together, we can find the liberation we need, whether that is more food or less, whether more generosity or the basic necessities, whether more security or more risk, whether forgiveness or the ability to forgive. And I hope that we can find liberation in faith and truth. That uncertainty will be a vibrant part of the searching and finding. That ultimately we will keep being steered by love and to love—the gritty kind that is in action, whether it feels fuzzy or not.

If you're wound tight, exhausted, sick, even dying, may you find the right mix of rest, courage and peace. If you feel like you're shriveled in soul, may you find the energy to search, to dig out of the rubble back out to life or to dig into the muck to find what is true.

If you're too certain, either congratulations, or may you find comfort with doubt (I'm not certain which). If you're too cynical, may you not dull yourself to the hopeful, beautiful part of truth.

You'll put this book down in a moment and return to grinding at your job or looking for a job, to cleaning up an oil slick, to hating cancer, whether yours or someone else's. Whatever it is you return to, I hope you find yourself with people who love you and welcome your love.

If you find answers, may you share them with the rest of us—but reluctantly and humbly so we can listen. (If you have certainty, make it the kind of faith and not of bludgeoning.) Shout it if you have to, but there's so much blustery shouting already that it's better to avoid association with that embarrassing crowd. And then share your next answers when the first ones change or adjust (I presume mine will). I probably don't want to hear your unified theory on exactly who God is and the meaning of everything, but I'm interested in how you find God present (or not) in your life.

Just like this our hearts can break together and we can find a little less loneliness, which isn't little at all, and a lot more justice. We shouldn't turn away from suffering, but neither should we gorge on it like vultures/angels. Whether or not we believe in miracles today, we can believe that in helping each other something miraculous happens—even something mystical. Christ might be present.

I dislike the word—and idea—*blessed*. It always presumes that some get the blessing and others do not. I don't want to believe in a God or world that works that way, though it's hard to deny it.

For example, I'm standing here now with Mike, two days out of the hospital. He's laughing. With concentrated bravado he starts a wrestling match with me, though I have to be careful. He's so slight it seems moving my thumb too fast could throw him across the room.

If we believe in God, what do we say about Mike and his family, about a boy who was cursed by cancer and then saved by the earthquake that killed 230,001? Saying he's blessed seems absurd in one way (for what it says about God); saying he's not blessed seems absurd in another (for being ungrateful that he's somehow alive).

For you in Haiti, forgive us that we don't love you as much as we love ourselves. Not even close. It is complex and hard work to help well now and for the future, but that's a challenge, not an excuse. May the help you need come as quickly as possible—through your own courage and creativity, as well as through the right and generous responses of others.

How can we claim blessing as people are suffering so profoundly right now? And how is it possible *not* to be incredibly grateful for each day Mike has to live—receiving love and giving joy to people around him (as now he zooms Matchbox cars around on the floor)?

I don't know. Honest faith has to admit that it makes no sense. But maybe it's not a bad thing to be left echoing what a father prayed for his son's healing two thousand years ago: "I believe; help my unbelief." Then we can hope that together we'll hear Jesus' gentle answer, "Blessed are those who have not seen and yet have come to believe."

With every crisis of faith, what we believe is crucified, and then we wait expectantly, whether in defeat or in joyful hope, to see what part of our faith is resurrected.

◆ ◆ ◆

As I get ready to drive to the airport for a red-eye flight back to Florida, the family wants to pray together. Gustave, Michelette, Carla, Djenika, Mike and I stand in a circle. I'm holding hands with Carla and Mike. It's baffling, all the sorrow and generosity that led to this good moment. So many lost and a few found.

I guess it's too much to try to hold all the sorrow and joy, uncertainty and hope, questions and anger and peace, all of it in every moment. There are many reasons to cry, though I still haven't broken down and wept yet. Right now rain is pouring down on so many Haitians still homeless long after the earthquake. Right now somewhere an innocent child is crying out futilely for someone human or divine to stop what is happening to her. Right now somewhere else someone is losing the fight with cancer. Right now you could easily write a detailed list about those around you.

For Mike, his oncologist says if the leukemia comes back he'll only have a 20 percent chance of surviving. But right now, right now, right now . . . where I am right now, standing with this family, it is pure gratitude. It has to be. It can be nothing else standing with Mike's smile, with their thankfulness for all that has happened, with their faith, with the chance to share in their joy.

There are other moments when the reality of hope and faith seems as true as—yes, maybe even truer than—the reality of uncertainty and suffering. There are no guarantees, but these ephemeral glimpses seem to point to something about love that is eternal.

For the moment, I just hold onto Mike's tiny hand and pray.

◆ ◆ ◆

And so, finally, God, all of this is to you, only you.

May you accept it with all of its doubt and anger and self-righteousness and protests. This book is my psalm to you, clawing its way toward faith and gratitude.

May you accept my muck-stained love.

May you accept my clogged-up tears and maybe turn them to water.

May you teach me to sing like Enel and others did in that all-night vigil as they and their city laid there bruised and broken.

May I keep finding you in the rubble—the body of Christ broken for us.

May those who are suffering especially, and yet even all of us, keep finding you on this shaky planet—the body of Christ with us.

May we, somehow, keep becoming the body of Christ, that your distance would come nearer.

I want to be vulnerable to faith, hope and love. Vulnerable to your salvation. Committed to following you. And vulnerable to truth and however that might change my faith.

Vulnerable to your love, so do not hide your face from us—that we may not be able to hide our faces from you.

Amen.

READING GROUP GUIDE

K ENT ANNAN'S BOOK very personally explores some of life's big questions—faith, doubt and suffering. For Annan, the reason for taking on these subjects is the devastating earthquake in Haiti, where he has been working for eight years. But the same questions about suffering and uncertainty are relevant to each of our lives wherever we live—whether in relation to a cancer diagnosis, a child's accident, the suffering of a loved one, the poverty so many people face around the world or a million other occasions. Many of us face crises of faith at different times. Can we make it through these "after shocks" without denying either reality (in both its beauty and cruelty) or God? This is an honest, engaging—and ultimately hopeful—look at a difficult subject. We hope you'll find *After Shock* meaningful in your own search for honest faith.

1. Do you find it hard or easy to discuss the big questions about God? Explain.

2. What kinds of events—whether they happened to you or to someone you know, or on a large scale like 9/11 or an earthquake—have caused you to feel something like "spiritual aftershocks"? Explain.

3. Which kind of suffering do you find it hardest to understand—what is caused by nature ("acts of God") or by humans (people's cruelty to each other)? Why?

4. Kent lists (in "An Annotated Wish List," right before the chapter "Accept Uncertainty") some changes he would propose for God. What do you think of writing something like that down? What would be on your own list of how you'd like to see God work

differently in the world? And why do you think God didn't do differently the things on Kent's list and your own?

5. What are the clichés about God that you find yourself or people around you using? (Kent discusses a few in the chapter "Spiritual Aftershocks.") What element of truth do they have? Why are they inadequate? What would be better to say instead?

6. Kent writes that he considers this more a psalm than a theological book about suffering, faith and doubt. What is the difference between a psalm or poem and something that tries to explain the answers? Does it make a difference in how you read if the author isn't claiming to "answer" the problem but is trying instead to wrestle honestly with the questions?

7. How can a personal crisis of faith or questions about suffering lead us toward working for more justice?

8. Kent is a Christian—but he expresses that some days he also feels like an atheist or an agnostic, or in conflict with or indifferent toward God. What do you think of talking about faith like this? Can you identify with having faith (or lack of it) that varies in a similar way?

9. Kent mentions a few of the most meaningful psalms to him. Discuss which psalms—or poems, songs or books—are most meaningful to you on the topics of faith/doubt/God and why.

10. Do you experience God as near? Do you experience God as distant? How?

11. Have you ever left your faith—and if so, did you come back to it? Why or why not? If you did return to your faith, what helped bring you back, and how was your faith different?

12. Is Jesus part of suffering for you? Kent prays to Jesus on the cross and Jesus gone from the cross (in the chapter "Jesus [Crucifix Versus Cross]"). Do you find Jesus most connected to our lives when you consider him (a) *with us in* our suffering or (b) as the one who *rescues us from* our suffering?

13. Kent writes that his search is for "honest faith." Do you ever encounter in yourself or in others something that seems like less-than-honest faith? How would you define "honest faith"?

About the Author

KENT ANNAN is author of *Following Jesus Through the Eye of the Needle* and codirector of Haiti Partners. He began working in Haiti in 2003 after previously working with refugee ministries in western Europe, Albania and Kosovo. A graduate of Princeton Theological Seminary, he now travels regularly to Haiti from Florida, where he lives with his wife, Shelly, and their children, Simone and Cormac. One hundred percent of the author's proceeds from this book go to education in Haiti through Haiti Partners.

For more about Kent, his work with Haiti Partners and his books:

www.KentAnnan.com
www.HaitiPartners.com
facebook.com/kentannan
twitter.com/kentannan

ABOUT THE COVER

MY WIFE AND I ATTENDED this church a dozen times when we first moved to Haiti in 2003. Only the front wall was left standing after the January 2010 earthquake. It's devastating for that church community, most of whom also lost their homes in this town. And as you move through rubble like this, it's hard to not occasionally be struck by the question: in suffering—whether on a catastrophic scale or something very personal—which part of our faith stays standing?

This question is relevant in rural Haiti, in suburban America and anywhere in between.

A few seconds after my friend took this photo, several kids came riding through that church door on a donkey. Then later when we came by, some kids were playing back just behind this wall. The foundation was all that was left—and it was perfect for kicking around a patched-up, half-deflated soccer ball. We went and played (and laughed) with them. Life goes on even after your world crashes. Life goes on in the midst of suffering. If we're still going to believe, then one of the questions is how to have honest faith along the way.

ABOUT
Following Jesus Through the Eye of the Needle

KENT ANNAN left behind his comfortable life in the United States to face the world beyond its gates. In *Following Jesus Through the Eye of the Needle* you'll vividly enter into Annan's adventure of moving to Haiti—beginning when he and his wife moved into a tin-roofed, no-electricity, no-running-water home with a Haitian family. Ultimately you'll be inspired to search after God in uncharted territory on a path that may lead to your local soup kitchen—or to the other side of the world. It's an unflinchingly honest look at love and service, and the stumbles and joys along the way.

"Filled with the hope that there is a God who can set free both the oppressed and the oppressors."

SHANE CLAIBORNE,
bestselling author and activist

"This wonderful book is as much about faith and commitment and service and love and love of service as it is about the author and about Haiti. Please read it. You will be uplifted and you will be inspired, but most of all you will enjoy it."

EDWIDGE DANTICAT,
author of *Brother, I'm Dying* and National Book Award finalist

LIKEWISE. *Go and do.*

A man comes across an ancient enemy, beaten and left for dead. He lifts the wounded man onto the back of a donkey and takes him to an inn to tend to the man's recovery. Jesus tells this story and instructs those who are listening to "go and do likewise."

Likewise books explore a compassionate, active faith lived out in real time. When we're skeptical about the status quo, Likewise books challenge us to create culture responsibly. When we're confused about who we are and what we're supposed to be doing, Likewise books help us listen for God's voice. When we're discouraged by the troubled world we've inherited, Likewise books encourage us to hold onto hope.

In this life we will face challenges that demand our response. Likewise books face those challenges with us so we can act on faith.

likewisebooks.com